Expectant Entrepreneur
How to Grow a Business and a Baby

Claire Navaro Krawsczyn

Expectant
Entrepreneur

How to Grow a Business and a Baby

Claire Navaro Krawsczyn

NEW DEGREE PRESS

COPYRIGHT © 2020 CLAIRE NAVARO KRAWSCZYN

EXPECTANT ENTREPRENEUR

How to Grow a Business and a Baby

ISBN   978-1-63676-525-9 *Paperback*

            978-1-63676-063-6 *Kindle Ebook*

            978-1-63676-064-3 *Ebook*

This book is dedicated to Adam, who made it all possible.
To my girls, who made it all worth it.
And to all of my family, by birth and by choice,
who have supported me along the way.

"There is no one way to live, love, raise children, arrange a family, run a school, a community, a nation. The norms were created by somebody, and each of us is somebody. We can make our own normal."

—GLENNON DOYLE, *UNTAMED*

Contents

Introduction

———

Pregnant.

The pregnancy test almost seemed smug, sitting there on my bathroom vanity. Its job was complete: tell me whether or not my suspicions of pregnancy were correct. They were, and I was.

The pace at which my mind went from overwhelming joy at the news I was expecting my second baby to straight overwhelmed at everything I had to accomplish before she arrived was lightning fast. The pregnancy test had hardly dried before I dove into business owner mindset. Although my husband, Adam, and I had discussed having another child and were open and ready to grow our family, there was still an element of shock when it happened.

While on a weekend getaway to the beach to celebrate our good news, Adam and I stopped in a bookstore. I looked for a book to give me insights about how to do exactly what I was doing: growing a business and a baby.

There were no books on the shelves at the local bookstore. I figured the lack of resources was simply due to reduced inventory, but a quick Google search told a different story. I found a few articles about entrepreneurship and family, but nothing that really gave me insights as to what was in store for me or things to think about during the next nine to ten months. I found plenty of resources about family planning, how to prepare for a maternity leave in a corporate situation, and how to find "work-life balance" as a working mom. But there was a gap in the market.

As I worked through my list of things to consider, budgets to crunch, clients to communicate with, and team members to train, I searched for more information. I wanted to hear the real, raw stories of women who were growing amazing businesses, supporting their families, *and also* giving themselves the space and time to be a new mother. I wanted to know how women planned for a maternity leave when, in reality, they were still an essential player in their daily work. All the advice I heard was amazing and wonderful and inspirational, but it wasn't realistic to my situation:

- Build a bigger team
- Take yourself out of the daily grind
- Remove yourself from client interactions
- Outsource, outsource, outsource
- Create all the systems for all the things

The truth was I really *wanted* to do all of these things. But by the time I found out I was pregnant, sat with the news, and planned for an early December arrival (plus or minus a couple of weeks), I had about six months to do everything I

felt like I needed to do. Many of the advice articles I found online were highly applicable to venture-funded startups with loads of cash and resources and larger teams. I couldn't find many stories of women in my shoes: small businesses with fewer than ten people involved in which every dollar impacted my take-home pay.

I did not have a maternity leave built into my still-growing business. I did not have a partner who was financially providing for our family. I had several team members who relied on my monthly retainer payments to support their own lives. I bought my own insurance, managed my client roster, and generated all of the sales for my business. How was I going to also give myself the space to nurture this other role as mother in the way I really wanted to?

It occurred to me then, for better or for worse, that I could fill that gap with my own story, and that maybe there were other women out there would like to know that 1) it's possible to be great at both roles and 2) they're not alone at a time that can feel very lonely and stressful. I could share my own experience of having two children while being self-employed, and I could gather the stories of other women around me going through this phase of life. That very day, while standing at a bookstore off the beach in North Carolina, the *Expectant Entrepreneur* project was born.

I started talking with women who had previously been in my position. I started asking to speak to women—many of them strangers whose stories I found online slightly resembled mine—and I asked questions. *What did this feel like for*

you? How did you handle it? Why does it feel so hard? Did you ever feel lonely?

The stories I heard changed everything for me. I realized I was selling myself a sob story that wasn't true. I wasn't a lone unicorn with no one else who understood my situation. I was one of many, many fierce women who are amazing mothers and successful business owners. We're a brilliant and massive herd of unicorns who know *exactly what it feels like.*

Expectant Entrepreneur is a look at these women who shared their stories about being entrepreneurs and mothers and the beautiful collision of the two. Through the stories of women who have successfully done both, who are working through it right now, or who plan to take on both the entrepreneur and mother identities down the road, I'm exploring what it means to be an Expectant Entrepreneur: a woman who wants more out of life, more out of her business, and more out of herself.

Though I have my own experience to lean on, the best lessons came from the stories of other women. The following pages are my vision for my own contribution to the Expectant Entrepreneur community.

The goal now is to offer my thoughts as a way for other women to check their own. In no way is my experience comprehensive of every other woman's journey. That is impossible. Our paths through motherhood and through business ownership will be uniquely interesting. But what *is* possible is simply to share my experience and offer reflections on my lessons learned in the event they help even just one other business

owner navigate this specific, beautiful, complicated, and stressful time.

I start this narrative by setting the scene: how did we get to this place in history in which women can even share their journeys as business owners? Decades of women have carved their paths on their own, helping create a society and an economy in which women are able to follow their passions and start their own businesses. Our community of Expectant Entrepreneurs really began decades ago: with my mother, her mother, and countless other women who raised bold women who pushed boundaries.

This book is a simple reminder to any woman who is building her business and growing her family that *you are not alone.* We are out there, and we know what it feels like to be in your shoes. You deserve to be celebrated, and you CAN do this. Your business will thrive, and you will be the mother that you wish to be. We're here for you. Welcome to the Expectant Entrepreneur community.

Part 1

How We Got Here

1

The Evolution of Women's Roles

———

"You can be anything that you want to be."

I remember hearing those words on repeat when I was a young girl growing up in Cincinnati, Ohio. We lived in a great neighborhood that featured hilly streets lined with trees. My childhood best friend and I would pop tar bubbles on the street during the summer and spend hours playing with Barbies during the winter. There were neighborhood bike rides, and you could pack in a decently distanced adventure, so long as you were sure you would make it back home before the street lights turn on.

The feeling of being anything I wanted to be was both consuming and freeing. As an adult, I remember calling my mom from my parked car in the grocery store parking lot.

"If I can be anything, how do I choose what to be?"

This freedom to choose was hugely overwhelming to me. I couldn't articulate it at the time, but I was feeling the pressure to make the most out of the opportunities before me. There was a tension between choosing the right path for me as a creative individual and the path of highest potential.

I remember the litany of *shoulds* that played in my head: I should be mother, I should be a wife, I should be financially independent, I should be a career woman, I should pursue my dreams, I should be fit and in shape, I should be well-educated. In my young years as a sixteen- or seventeen-year-old, I was picking colleges out of a book based on what I thought I should be. As a young graduate, I was picking careers that should lead me down the path of most potential.

At the time, I didn't quite comprehend what a huge advantage I had as a privileged, white, highly educated woman. I was born in 1986, which feels significantly further in the past than appropriate (the thought of telling my daughters when I was born already makes me cringe!).

The change from my mom's generation—she was born in 1956—to my own is significant when it comes to the possibilities for women's futures and professional careers. My mom, Kim, was a nurse for the majority of her career. As she remembers it, growing up as the oldest of five siblings in Cincinnati, she had limited options.

"At the time, college was not an option for me, and I think it was primarily because my dad didn't believe that he could afford to send us all," she said. "Getting a loan to go to school was also not an option for me. I decided to go to nursing

school, and I graduated after three years with a diploma, which was the minimum requirement to sit the boards."

My mom married my dad in 1977, and she continued to pursue her education during the evenings and weekends until my older brother, Tim, was born in 1982. More than two decades later, when my mom was in her forties, she returned to her education and achieved her dream of having a college degree. She continued her career as a nurse and excelled at her work. My younger sister, Erin, was born in 1991, and my mom continued to work and raise us. When my sister was in third grade, my mom stopped working.

"Dad and I had a lot of conversations about our household and how we would raise you kids," my mom said. "Ultimately, the cost of my pursuing my career was going to make our life more complicated. I was experiencing some burnout, too, and it felt like the right thing for me to stay home and focus on raising our family."

My mom may not have seen the direct impact her experience had on me, but in the years after she stopped working as a nurse, her own exploration and entrepreneurial side emerged. I witnessed her seek and achieve her real estate license, fitness instructor certification, and achieve a Master Gardener designation in the state of Ohio. She volunteered constantly and was always finding new ways to fulfill her own interests outside of being a mother. Her ambition to find a new direction in her life always felt full of exploration and curiosity, and looking back, I think it helped me to see the power in pursuing passions—and moving on if one didn't fill you with joy.

Not until my early adulthood did I realize how intentional my parents were when they told my siblings and me that we could be anything we wanted to be when we grew up. My sister and I had the same opportunities afforded to us as our older brother. My parents shucked the "acceptable" paths of nurse or teacher or housewife and, instead, invested heavily in our education, supported every whim, and drove us across the country to explore any higher education institute that held our attention. Again, my privilege is not lost on me: we had the world open to us, and we could be anything we wanted to be.

This encouragement is not unique to my family, and it's relevant to the path of many women entrepreneurs today. I didn't just wake up one day in a society that accepted women as business owners. The fact that *Expectant Entrepreneur* exists is due to decades of women who pushed boundaries, juggled family demands, searched for their own identities, both within and outside of the home, and raised daughters who felt confident enough to pursue their passions. The history goes back to well before my lifetime and before my mom's, too.

After World War II, women were solidified as part of the American workforce. As the American Dream kicked in and subdivisions sprawled, there was the need for more income to support the new lifestyle. Women became part of the working world, and not just in the style of Rosie the Riveter. Nursing and educational career paths were two of the more acceptable "nurturing careers" permitted by higher education institutions. In fact, until 1972 when Title IX was passed, colleges and universities could legally keep women

from enrolling in selected degree fields, like engineering and chemistry.[1]

Women's roles quickly expanded from those "nurturing careers." The 1970s and 1980s saw huge surges in the women's rights movement. During these decades, the initial women's liberation movement, which focused on women's right to vote, coincided with second-wave feminism, which sought women's liberation in more areas than voting alone, like politics, work, the family, and sexuality.[2] There was a nationwide push to pass the Equal Rights Amendment, which, despite the initial success, incited a very successful STOP ERA campaign that slowed its passage across the nation, even to this day.[3] Overall, the United States was experiencing forward momentum, and the growth of feminism continued to move women's roles forward, breaking the barriers to enter into the workforce outside of nursing and education.

By the time I was born in the 1980s, women were a much stronger force in the economy. Women were proudly taking over jobs traditionally held by men, and according to research, women's share of professional jobs increased from 44 percent in 1972 to 49 percent in 1985. In that same time,

---

1   "Why Are So Many Teachers Women?," National Women's History Museum, accessed April 11, 2020.

2   *Encyclopaedia Britannica Online*, s.v. "Women's Rights Movement," accessed October 11, 2020.

3   Wilfred U. Codrington III and Alex Cohen, "The Equal Rights Amendment Explained," Brennan Center, January 23, 2020, accessed October 11, 2020.

women's share of "management jobs" (think: leadership positions) nearly doubled from 20 to 36 percent.[4]

With the development of technology that made housework less time-intensive and more widespread acceptance of women's roles as income-earners and professionals, women's trajectory into the workforce has continued to move upward with every passing year.

The cost of this expansion into the workforce came in the household. As women's careers moved forward, the strain on homes and families became an increasing source of stress, particularly for the women who were trying to "have it all."

In 1989, Arlie Russell Hochschild published her groundbreaking text, *The Second Shift: Working Parents and the Revolution at Home*.[5] In her research on American families, Hochschild explored the household work that women in dual-career families took on at home: laundry, cooking, cleaning, childcare, and more. This exploration of the existing demands at work and home helped to identify the tension and pressure many working women feel.

Part-time work grew more appealing, as did roles in which women held more control over their hours and time allotted. Real estate is a great example. In the early 1900s, women began pursuing careers in real estate as a way to make money in a safer environment than factory work. During World War

---

4   George Guildern, "Women in the Work Force," *The Atlantic*, September 1986.

5   Arlie Hochschild and Anne Machung, *The Second Shift: Working families and the revolution at home* (New York: Penguin, 2012).

II, progress in real estate stalled as women got pulled back into factory work, but after the war, women turned to the industry again. By 1978, the majority of the National Association of Realtors (NAR) members were women. By 1980, almost 300,000 women were real estate agents, making up 45 percent of the industry.[6]

Real estate is just one example. In the 1980s, many aspects of the working world seemed to converge. Women's earnings were needed in homes across the country. Society started to accept women as professionals, and new opportunities for income expanded. At the same time, household demands continued to fall largely on women's shoulders, creating a need for increased flexibility and control over when, where, and how they worked. The drive for entrepreneurial endeavors increased, and women's role as business owners saw a huge leap forward.

"From knitting mittens to selling real estate and writing software packages for personal computers, more and more women are working for themselves, launching small businesses in their homes. From 1972 to 1982, the percentage of self-employed workers in nonagricultural industries who are women rose from 26 to 32."[7]

Entrepreneurship was growing as a viable option for women. Then, in 1988, Congress passed the Women's Business Ownership Act, which ended discrimination in lending and made

6   Grace Stetson, "The Untold History Behind Why Most Real Estate Agents Are Women," *Apartment Therapy*, March 30, 2019.
7   George Guildren, "Women in the Work Force," *The Atlantic*, September 1986.

it illegal for lenders to require married women to get their husband's signature for loans (can you imagine?).[8] It also allowed women-owned businesses to compete for government contracts.

Networking groups, support systems, and organizations for educating women entrepreneurs began to pop up on the scene. Women could train themselves, find like-minded peers, and expand their interests and skills in the context of business ownership. Women were starting to see more women business owners on the rise, and the momentum was confirmed when President George H. W. Bush appointed Susan Engeleiter to be the first woman to head the Small Business Administration in 1989.

The downturn of the economy in the late 1980s and early 1990s created a greater sense of urgency and necessity around women entrepreneurship. With the dawn of the Internet and the growing reality of online businesses, women-led startups saw a surge of growth at two to four times the general startup rate.[9] In addition, major women entrepreneurs were taking center stage in homes across the nation. It was the era of Martha Stewart and Oprah, and women were listening.

As the Internet became increasingly user-friendly, funding became more widely available, and support and resources became more prolific, the population of women business owners has continued to rise year after year. According to

8   "Public Law 100-533, Women's Business Ownership Act of 1988," *Annual review of population law* 15 (1988): 174.

9   Debrah Lee Charatan, "30 Years of Female Entrepreneurship: From Anomalies To Assets," *Entrepreneur.com*, May 4 2016.

an article in the *Harvard Business Review*, "The number of women in business has been steadily rising over the past twenty years. Hundreds of women-owned businesses are sprouting up every single day, bringing with them new jobs, a positive influx in the local economies, and a strengthening of the communities they exist within."[10]

Women-owned businesses grow by nearly 1,821 net new women-owned businesses every day. There are 12.3 million women-owned businesses as of January 2017. We employ 9 million people and generate more than $1.8 TRILLION in revenue every year.[11]

Women-owned businesses account for almost 40 percent of all US businesses.

WE ARE A FORCE.

---

10 Jackie VanderBrug, "The global rise of female entrepreneurs," *Harvard Business Review* 4 (2013).

11 Elaine Parker, "Women Entrepreneurs are on the Rise," *The Hill*, January 19, 2019.

2

The Challenge of Women's Entrepreneurship

———

Work flexible hours!

Experience unlimited income potential!

You are your own boss!

Spend more time with family!

Work from anywhere!

Say yes to only the projects you love!

These phrases are familiar to anyone who has ever considered starting their own business, and it's the mantra I said to myself over and over as I sat at my computer at 2:00 a.m., scraping together the final words for a client's branding project. I sat with my dog , Avon Barksdale, who was happy to keep me company and snoozing soundly at my feet in my

third-floor office space. I was in my second year of business, and I was making solid, real money.

I'd fully replaced my income from my professional job that I left in 2013. My house was quiet. Adam, my husband, was sleeping soundly downstairs, preparing for his own day at work at the University of Cincinnati. I was hungry for work and to make my business a success. I said yes to nearly every job that came my way, and I worked early mornings and late nights to make it happen.

At the time, it was exciting. I had the energy and focus of a twenty-seven-year-old with no children, no health issues, and a stable bank account. Staying up late was not something I did all the time, but I certainly had the option to do so. I had my struggles then, but life was simpler.

I was making enough money to feel secure, but not so much that I couldn't balance my own books or take control of my cash flow. My days were filled with networking, coffee meetings, and lunchtime conversations. I took breaks to exercise, caught a nap or two when I needed one, and popped right up to my office after Adam and I ate dinner to finish a day's worth of work. Growth was happening, and it felt great. My microbusiness was working well, and I was bright-eyed about the future.

My business turned from side gig to this "real" business when I got my first big yes.

The year was 2012, and I had just gotten married. We were living in Connecticut, and had recently moved from

Washington, DC, so Adam could pursue a career opportunity. Without my previous Baltimore-to-DC commute, I had at least four more hours back in my day—and even more if you took out the getting-ready time investment. With my full-time company's permission and a couple of signed no-conflict papers, I had picked up some hours working as a freelance writer. My largest client at the time was a wonderful woman-owned company based out of Virginia. I loved its mission and its service-based work, and a mutual connection had linked us up at the right time. This company was expanding its team and looking for contractors to support content creation with some highly lucrative and innovative clients.

"What would it take to get more Claire time?"

The question came after nearly six months of freelancing for the company at the respectable rate of $50 per hour. That rate, to me, felt appropriate but safe. It was side-hustle money. But they were asking the question I hadn't asked myself: what would it take for me to make the leap?

At that time, I was thinking about launching into freelance full time. My professional job was great, and I absolutely enjoyed the people I was working with. The industry was a tough one, and I knew it wasn't where I wanted to be forever. For the first time, I thought about what it might take to give more of me.

I would have to be available during the day to work on strategy and participate in client conversations instead of fitting in writing at night and on the weekends. I wrestled with the question, and for the first time, I actually considered what an

hourly rate reflected. It was experience and the work product. It was also potentially taxes, insurance, supplies, retirement, and more. The result was a big number—bigger than I really thought was possible, but it was the number I needed to hit to be self-sufficient.

I decided to put the number on the table and make an ask of nearly double my current rate with a guaranteed minimum set of hours per month.

They agreed—and when I got that yes, I knew my business was possible.

Most women business owners I know have their own version of this moment when everything felt aligned and exciting.

"I had a moment after we sold out at our very first farmers market," said Rachel DesRochers, owner of several gratitude-centered businesses, including Grateful Grahams, a nationally distributed line of homemade grahams and treats. "I knew then that we had a product that people wanted and that, with the work, it would be a success."

The numbers don't lie: more and more women are starting their own businesses every day. We believe we can do something different, or something better than the way it's being done, or we believe that we could do our jobs better if we had more control over the process and client relationships. There are amazing success stories of the victors.

Sara Blakely, owner of Spanx, went from being a door-to-door fax salesperson to the nation's youngest woman billionaire.

Sarah Kauss dropped her gig in real estate development to found the multimillion dollar stainless steel water bottle company S'well. Lisa Price founded Carol's Daughter, a multicultural beauty brand that started as a side project and was later acquired by L'Oreal. TheSkimm, a daily newsletter with millennial-friendly summaries of world news, was founded by twenty-something-year-old college friends Carly Zakin and Danielle Weisberg. The success of woman-founded companies is inspiring, but it doesn't paint the full picture of women in entrepreneurship.

The history of women entrepreneurs into the twenty-first century is not a story of "right place, right time." It is, rather, a history of creative problem-solving by generations of women who wanted to pursue independence at a time when independent women were not widely celebrated. My own business history may feel familiar to many women who start their own businesses in today's environment, but it took time, work, and sacrifice to get where we are today.

Entrepreneurship has not always been an avenue for women who simply want to see if they have what it takes to make it on their own. Rather, entrepreneurship was a necessity for many women, particularly those who worked in low-paying jobs or who had limited or no upward mobility within their own existing jobs. Launching their own businesses was a viable way, and often *the only* viable way, to change both income and personal satisfaction with their work.[12]

---

12   Stephanie Sarkis, "Gender Inequality Led to the Rise of Women Entrepreneurs," *Forbes*, March 5, 2019.

Since the 1980s, women in general have looked at business ownership for several critical reasons:

- To escape social constructs of female roles and responsibilities
- To create more control over her division of time and work-home structure
- To avoid or reduce workplace harassment or mistreatment

I found this research both inspiring and depressing. History paints a frustrating picture for women in business. The growth in woman entrepreneurship is fascinating and impressive. The first part of this book celebrates the rise of women as business owners, and this fact continues to be worthy of recognition. But as I researched more and learned about the reality of *why* women have historically moved to entrepreneurship, I felt more and more unsettled by how we, as women, got here in the first place.

Women face discrimination and harassment in the workplace.[13] The collective "we" were tired of carrying the pressures of workplace demands and the second shift of domestic work. We were facing growing childcare costs and limited childcare options.[14] The best choice, for thousands of women, was to leave the structure of a traditional work environment and go out on their own, making their own rules and taking all of the risks that came with it.

---

13   Liz Elting, "Why Women Quit," *Forbes*, October 21, 2019.

14   Caroline Castrillon, "Why Moe Women Are Turning to Entrepreneurship," *Forbes*, February 4, 2019.

If we put all of this information together, the story goes like this: A woman might face direct challenges in the workplace, like harassment, and chances are good (73 percent) that she is experiencing microaggressions or daily discrimination rooted in gender bias.[15] She earns less than her male colleagues, despite equal performance, and she experiences the motherhood penalty, which equates to losing 4 percent of her salary for every child she has, while her male counterparts receive a 6 percent increase in their salary for every child they have.[16]

After work, she heads home, and then takes on the second shift of household duties that are still primarily her responsibility. If she's expecting a child, she faces the reality that there's no federal policy requiring her employer to provide paid leave.[17] At the same time, the cost of childcare is growing rapidly across the country.[18] If she has that child and takes (possibly) unpaid time off to be with that child after birth, there's a chance she might never go back, as 43 percent of highly qualified women don't return to the workforce.[19] Instead, she may decide to take matters into her own hands and start a business of her own, joining the climbing statistics of women entrepreneurs.

---

15   Rachel Thomas, et al., *Women in the Workplace 2019: a Report by LeanIn and McKinsey & Company,* LeanIn.org, 2019, Accessed April 20, 2019.

16   Claire Cain Miller, "The Motherhood Penalty vs. the Fatherhood Bonus," *The Upshot (Blog), The New York Times,* September 6, 2014.

17   Miranda Bryant, "Maternity Leave: US Policy Is Worst on List of the World's Richest Countries," *The Guardian,* January 27, 2020.

18   Andrew Keshner, "Child-care costs in America have soared to nearly $10k per year," *MarketWatch,* March 8, 2019.

19   Paulette Light, "Why 43% of Women With Children Leave Their Jobs, and How to Get Them Back," *The Atlantic,* April 19, 2013.

And *that* is the bigger picture of the surge of mother entrepreneurs.

A global study by the National GEM Consortium examined women's perceived ability to start a business. In the United States and most of developed Europe, women are 18 percent less likely to think they can start their own business. In every economy across the world that was included in the study, women have lower perceptions of their entrepreneurial capabilities.[20]

Of those women who start their own businesses despite their reduced perception of their ability to do so, research shows that 90 percent of all women-owned businesses are sole proprietorships. The context around this fact is worth noting, particularly when it comes to financials. Woman-led ventures were 63 percent *less likely* to receive funding despite having equal ability as men-led ventures to achieve next-level objectives (i.e., IPO exits).[21] This number changes dramatically when you look to women of color, who are the fastest growing subset of female entrepreneurs in the country. Since 2007, the number of businesses launched by Black women has grown by 167 percent.[22]

With all other factors, like credit scores, held equal, minority women are denied loans and pay higher interest rates than

20 Jackie VanderBrug. "The Global Rise of Female Entrepreneurs," *Harvard Business Review,* September 4, 2013.

21 Shama Hyder, "State Of Women And Entrepreneurship 2020: Here's What You Need To Know," *Forbes,* March 10, 2020.

22 Ellen Sheng, "This underfunded female demographic is launching the most start-ups in America, far from Silicon Valley," *CNBC.com,* February 25, 2020.

white women, and in the world of venture capital, companies led by women of color receive less than 1 percent of all VC funding. Nearly 66 percent of *all* women report having trouble funding their businesses despite feeling more empowered in business today than they did five years ago.[23]

Women who start their own businesses are largely relying on their own skills and their own finances to do so.[24]

But who are the women who are willing to take the jump, start their businesses, and build their families? What does it take to become an Expectant Entrepreneur? Not all women *want* to have their own businesses, of course. But for those women who have the thought or inkling of an idea, they need to be willing to take the step to explore it further. Women need a particular mindset to leave the perceived security of a traditional job and start their own business. They need fortitude and willingness to tolerate risk to add a business to their domestic and family desires and responsibilities. They need to tap into what they want for themselves.

---

23 "Visa 2020 State of Female Entrepreneurship Report," *Visa,* February 2020, 6.

24 Robert Goffee and Richard Scase, *Women in Charge: The Experiences of Female Entrepreneurs* (New York: Routledge, 1985), 5.

3

Distinction: Mompreneurs & Mother-Entrepreneurs

———

Mompreneur. She-EO. Boss Babe. These phrases and terms have seen a dramatic rise in popularity over the past several decades as women's roles in business and executive positions of power have changed. Although *Expectant Entrepreneur* explores a specific subset of women as mother-entrepreneurs, I want to address why "mompreneurs" is not a phrase used in this book.

There are no hard and fast rules about who is, and who is not, a mother-entrepreneur. I am not in any way placing judgment on a woman's ability to refer to herself however she pleases. For the sake of clarity in this book, I refrained from using the phrase "mompreneur" as a way to describe entrepreneurs who are mothers.

Most of the women featured in this book, myself included, are equal or primary providers in their homes. They often choose to work more than forty hours a week. They are not

hobby business owners or making extra cash on the side through gigs or very part-time work. Rather, they are invested heavily—emotionally, and in many cases financially—in the success and growth of their business because it is important to them and makes them proud.

By definition, a mompreneur is a woman who sets up and runs her own business in addition to caring for her young child or children.[25] With time and more widespread use, mompreneur as a term has come to reflect different subsets of mother-entrepreneurs. At its core, a mompreneur is a mother who is an entrepreneur. Following this definition, Mompreneur® Showcase Group Inc. in Canada seeks to "support, educate, and empower moms in business." Investopedia, on the other hand, defines mompreneurs as women who are primarily full-time caregivers to their children and run businesses on the margins.[26]

Many multilevel marketing companies specifically use "mompreneurs" in their marketing as a way to attract women and offer opportunities for them to make money at home.[27] There are also definitions of mompreneurs as women who specifically work as entrepreneurs of businesses that directly serve or sell to other mothers.[28] Some women find offense in the phrase, citing that it takes away from a woman's

25 Lexico Oxford Dictionary, Online Ed., s.v. "Mompreneur," accessed March 15, 2020.

26 Lucas Downey, "Mompreneur," Investopedia, August 21, 2018.

27 Kris Betts, "Mompreneurs: Working from home through social commerce," KVUE.com, July 7, 2017.

28 Sandy Abrams, "Mompreneurs: Products Made by Moms for Moms," The Blog, Huffington Post, December 6, 2017.

accomplishments by adding a component of biological sex to it.[29]

The point is, an entrepreneur is an entrepreneur, regardless of sex, gender, type of business, parental status, or other aspect of life. This book explores mother-entrepreneurs and the commonalities and shared experiences among us through the term Expectant Entrepreneur.

As a woman, I celebrate women in business as a critical part of our economy, and I celebrate women who choose to stay home to raise their families. I recognize with deep empathy those women who want to have children and cannot, as well as those women who choose not to have children. I celebrate the entrepreneurial ambitions of men with respect, and I embrace the decision of fathers who choose to stay home with their children. This book is about community, and I hope it serves its purpose.

---

29   Krystal, "Please Stop Calling Me a Mompreneur," *Daily Femme (blog)*, 2017.

4

The Unique Mindset of Expectant Entrepreneurs

———

Kate Torgersen took a life-changing business trip.

The mom of seven-month-old twins was traveling for four days as an employee of Clif Bar & Company. At the time, Torgersen was exclusively breastfeeding her twins, and traveling for four days took some significant planning and coordination. She worked hard to boost her supply before she left to ensure her twins would have plenty to eat while she was gone, pumped consistently throughout her trip, and then had to maneuver nearly two gallons (*this blows my low-supply mind!*) of breast milk past TSA agents on the trip home.

"It was a nightmare," Torgersen said during a Mom-Led Innovation and Entrepreneurship interview with IDEO.[30] "I had to educate every person along the way about what it meant

———

30 Kate Torgerson, "What Motherhood Taught this CEO About Starting a Business," Interview by IDEO, May 6, 2020.

to be a nursing mom, and then I had to explain why I had coolers of milk with me on my flight home."

That experience of trying to store milk in hotel mini-fridges, interrupting meetings to pump, deftly trying to pack it in stainless steel bottles for the trip home, and hoping the milk stayed fresh until she could get it back to her twins served as the experience that tipped Torgersen over the edge into new product innovation. On the flight home, Torgersen started thinking: there has to be another way.

"Moms have grit," Torgersen said. "We just are willing to work hard."

Torgersen is the founder of Milk Stork, the first and only breast milk travel solution for working moms. She developed the idea for her best-selling product on the flight home, and within months, Milk Stork was being sought by major US companies as a new employee benefit for working and traveling mothers.

Torgersen's message of "moms have grit" is a sentiment that every entrepreneur I spoke with for this book expressed, though each expressed it in her own way:

Agility. Nimbleness. Pivoting. Persistence. Rebound. Seeker. Creator. Innovator. Flexibility. Curiosity. Fortitude. Stubbornness. Bravery.

The more women I spoke with, the stronger my suspicion became that mother-entrepreneurs are more alike than we

are different, and there's something unique about the mindset of business owners who are mothers, too.

The title of the book, *Expectant Entrepreneur,* was inspired by my own experience of having both of my daughters while simultaneously growing my business. But the phrase has come to mean much more to me than simply a description of a moment in time. I believe I was an Expectant Entrepreneur when I started my company in 2013, and that today—although I'm not planning on having any more children—I'm still an expectant entrepreneur.

History tells us that women have been consistently using entrepreneurship as a tool to enhance their lives. The women who broke barriers, who established businesses when society said they should stay home and could not compete in a business world, and who thought to themselves, "there has to be a better way," are all Expectant Entrepreneurs. They looked at the world around them, and they held it to a higher standard. They expected more from their experience as mothers and workers and leaders.

The literal definition of expectant is "having or showing an excited feeling that something is about to happen, especially something pleasant and interesting." That feeling is at the root of so many stories of entrepreneurism AND so many stories of motherhood.

In our businesses, we work with dedication and commitment because we know, at our core, there are many ways to solve the same problem. For Milk Stork and Kate Torgersen, the solution was about supporting breastfeeding mothers who

don't accept that you can't be both a breastfeeding mother and a traveling employee at the same time. We raise our standards of acceptance, and the idea that there's only one way for a problem to be solved is borderline heresy.

The entire reason many businesses are formed is simply because we expect things to be better or different, and as we work to build those solutions, the feeling that *something* is about to happen pushes us forward. The change, whether it's the dream of leaving a negative work environment, making more money, solving a problem in front of us, or building a better future, serves as momentum to put in the time, resources, risk, and work. We become entrepreneurs *because* we are expectant women—women who expect more than what we have—and we're okay with being bold about it.

In our families, the expectant phases are often filled with a slew of emotions and anticipation. The journey of going from no children to the first is life-changing, and every child after adds a new layer of anticipation and growth. We volunteer our bodies as hosts or, when that isn't an option, we pivot. We envision our family's future and we nurture our babies.

Pregnancy doles out its complications, physically and emotionally, and yet we power through and look back on the experience as a journey that forever changed who we are as women, mothers, partners, and—yes—as business owners. The expectant phase of motherhood is sometimes indescribable, as thoughts and concerns and worries swirl. The good news? The eagerness, the joy, and the love triumph.

The anticipation of *more* or *different* is at the core of an Expectant Entrepreneur.

The stories of the women in this book and my examination of my own experience as an Expectant Entrepreneur are what happen when we combine these two expectant phases of our lives: the phase of building a business and also growing our families.

Entrepreneurs of all genders and backgrounds can point to the time in their careers or in their lives when they had that moment when everything came together—the situation in which they took a perceived failure or problem and turned it into a massive success. Parents of all genders look to parenthood with expectancy, emotions, and anticipation. But the combination of these two things—the expectancy of an entrepreneur through the eyes of a mother OR the expectancy of a mother through the eyes of an entrepreneur—creates a new identity all together.

"There's research that shows that this idea of a 'mommy brain' is actually true," said Megan Flatt, a business consultant who helps women "run their business like a mother," a catchphrase she lived up to fully in our conversations. "Our physical body changes, and we all have that in common. We honestly come out of pregnancy as different women."

Megan is right. Science has proven that the gray matter of women's brains is changed by the hormones that are part of

pregnancy.[31] In fact, women's brains are altered so much that researchers are able to look at scans of a woman's brain alone and determine if she has had a child. Our brains' gray matter shrinks during the process, which is why women often report feeling foggy and having information recall issues during pregnancy, sloughing off unnecessary brain matter that our bodies deem no longer useful.

Elseline Hoekzema, lead researcher on the groundbreaking study of women's brains during and after pregnancy, noted that the loss of gray matter is an indication of maturation and specialization, suggesting that women become more able to focus and more attune to the needs of their child.[32] Once the baby has arrived, women's brains retain the changes, indicating long-term impact on the brains of child-bearing women.

"What that translates into is the idea that we're better able to emotionally connect to our children," Flatt said. "But also our clients and team members, too."

Rachel Murphy, a life coach and owner of Mindsettings coaching, has witnessed generations of business ownership and the entrepreneurial mindset. She grew up with entrepreneur parents, is married to a business owner, and runs multiple businesses of her own.

"Something that I watched my parents do, and in particular my mom, is keep pushing forward," Rachel said. "I think

---

31   Elseline Hoekzema et al, "Pregnancy leads to long-lasting changes in human brain structure," *Nature Neuroscience 20*, no 2 (February 2017): 287-296.

32   Ibid.

this 'go-go-go' mentality is something that entrepreneurs have in common."

Researchers in Madrid confirmed what many entrepreneurs believed to be true: our brains are wired differently. In a study, these researchers measured the brain activity of test groups that included entrepreneurs and non-entrepreneurs alike. The tests, which focused primarily on decision-making tasks, found that the brain activity of entrepreneurs was "significantly different [...]. Founders were quicker to respond and less inhibited. They quickly absorbed and embraced the problem, despite [the problem's] ambiguity."[33]

Entrepreneurs are better able to embrace ambiguous problems more quickly and use simple rules to move forward:

"In these respects, it appears that founders' brains are wired differently. We expect this difference will be explained by a combination of factors: a genetic component, early development and learning, and adult experience in problem resolution and decision-making."[34]

So entrepreneurs' brains are different, and mothers' brains are different, too. Combining the research about changes to women's brains during and after bearing a child and the changes that seem to be consistent across entrepreneurs begs the question: are mother-entrepreneurs a distinctly different type of person, both biologically and physiologically?

---

33 Peter Bryant and Elena Ortiz Terán, "Entrepreneurs' Brains are Wired Differently," *Harvard Business Review*, December 19, 2013.

34 Ibid.

My research, my own experience, and my observations of the amazing mother-entrepreneurs I know would argue that we are, in fact, a group of women who view life differently and share so many wonderful and challenging traits in common. That we, as a whole, are beautifully distinct women who are ready to expect more from ourselves, from our experience in life, and from our experiences as expectant entrepreneurs.

5

Hallmarks and Emergent Themes

—————

"When I started my business (while working full time and doing a certification), over a year ago, gung ho doesn't even begin to describe how I felt. I felt like wonder woman. I knew what I was doing would change the world—life transformation, helping amazing women take their life and business to the next level—to create a life on THEIR TERMS, to give them FREEDOM…just give me the road map and I'll show you how quickly I can make this happen.

Forget about the new biz stats, I would defy them all.

And I did, for a while. I quit my full-time job so I could work on my biz (replacing in one day my monthly salary); I pivoted, I marketed, I was published, I got awesome clients, I ticked all the boxes while running to the next intervals barely looking back once I passed them.

Then life happened"[35]

Does this story sound familiar?

These lines, written and shared by Rachel Reva, a media strategist, success coach, and writer, could be my story or the story of the many other expectant entrepreneurs in this book.

If your brain works like mine, the natural next line is about being humbled—about stopping or being forced to stop, or being dealt a blow in your business or personal life. We see the greatness of what *could be* and the potential of everything we want to do—but then something happens to stop us in our tracks. In fact, I wrote a similar story within this book. But after speaking to dozens of women and hearing their stories and seeing how their lives are unfolding, I want to share something different.

I want to share a different hypothesis and a different perspective. The women I've met in my journey as an Expectant Entrepreneur and the women who shared their stories with me offer a different "and then" in this common story line.

Instead of being stopped or experiencing a debilitating challenge that derailed all of their plans for success, the next line in their stories is about things getting *even better*. Life happened, and things got even more exciting than they had allowed themselves to imagine. Yes, maybe more complicated or requiring more logistics and definitely with less sleep, but

---

35 Rachel Reva, "Confessions of a Pregnant Entrepreneur," *Thrive-Global,* August 1, 2018.

better. Enhanced. Enriched. Longer days and shorter nights, but fuller, deeper, and more fulfilling. Because the next line in the story of an Expectant Entrepreneur is a step toward satisfying the "expectant" aspect of our journeys when we get to "have it all"—a phrase that may strike eye rolls and panic in some, but in many ways captures the goal of an Expectant Entrepreneur.

We *want* to have work environments and situations we control. We *want* to have families that we can be present for and support through our businesses. We *want* careers that have unlimited potential.

These wants and desires are not unique to a specific subset of women. There are millions of women who want it all, and their paths to creating the lives they want are different and equally beautiful. This is not a situation of having it "better than" another mother or "more than" another business owner. It's about believing that what we want is possible and being willing to make it happen.

The science of earlier chapters in this book paints an interesting picture of this community of women. Historical, biological, and environmental factors have created societies and situations in which our ability to pursue our ambitions as mothers and entrepreneurs is possible and, in some ways, natural.

What makes the next line in Rachel's story and the story of so many mother-entrepreneurs possible is a set of characteristics and qualities that emerged as consistent among the women who volunteered their stories. Each of the hallmark

traits of these women seemed to have dual functionality: they are skills and talents that are not unique to this group alone, but they appear to serve this group of women in a particular way by being applicable in both business and motherhood.

The emergent ideas and themes could have originated via business or motherhood; regardless of where those characteristics began, they appear to be part of what these women have in common and a hint as to why we feel connected and bonded to other mother-entrepreneurs.

"I had these lovely supportive girlfriends that totally didn't get what I did," Megan Flatt said. "Many of my friends would reach out with great intention to know how my business was going, but then I could see the disconnect in their eyes. Many were stay-at-home moms or they had a more traditional job. I just really didn't have the community in which I could collaborate and commiserate. And I ended up taking that desire to connect with other women in similar positions and creating a business out of it. I noticed that when I would get on the phone with my clients who were in similar situations to me, we would all express the same feelings. I knew that we all needed to be together and able to share together."

The Characteristics of Expectant Entrepreneurs

In an effort to share together, I will try to delineate what brings us together in the first place. Mother-entrepreneurs all over the world work independently. Many find their own communities of like-minded women, or, if they can't find them, they create them.

What are the characteristics of successful mother-business owners? Below are the traits I observed in the women around me who are choosing the path of mother-business owners. There are many more, but these ten characteristics form the structure in which I will share the stories of women in this book:

- Momentum
- Curiosity
- Empathy
- Big-Picture Thinking
- Creativity
- Flexibility
- Focus
- Self-Awareness
- Resilience
- Risk Tolerance

Each of these aspects of mother-business owners is an observation, not a rule. But it's an observation many women share. It's what brings women across the world together: our ability to house these traits and learn how to "unsilo" our brains and our existence as people to ensure we're efficiently applying everything we know to all aspects of our lives, while simultaneously expecting more change, more adjustment, and more unknown.

Through these themes, I'll share the stories of women in locations as diverse as the United States, Australia, and Africa and show that despite many, many differences, we are all a larger part of a great community of Expectant Entrepreneurs—the women who come from a long history of mothers

who chose to divert from the clear paths, take a risk, and work hard to be the best business owners and mothers they can be at any given time on any given day.

Part 2

The Stories Inside

6

The Stories Inside

Clair Jones and Caroline Maurer are some of the lucky ones.

The two women co-own Witty Kitty Digital, a full-service digital marketing, social media, and website development agency. They also had babies about six months apart. As a duo who works remotely—Clair in Salt Lake City and Caroline in Portland, Maine—they built a partnership and a working system that changed fluidly with the ebbs and flows of parenthood.

"My pregnancy was sort of the test kitchen for our business," Clair said. "But we worked together to structure our business and then how we planned to run our business as new moms."

What Clair and Caroline had in their business is what many mother-entrepreneurs crave: a community of women who understand the experience of being a mother and an entrepreneur. This craving for women who understood my situation, who could look me in the eye and tell me that they truly understood what I was feeling, is something many mother-entrepreneurs seek.

"I jokingly referred to myself and some of my clients as 'moms in the middle,'" said Megan Flatt, owner of Let's Collective, a business growth strategy firm. "As entrepreneurs, we weren't mothers in the standard corporate situation. But we also weren't stay-at-home mothers, either. We straddled the pros and the cons of both identities."

Moms in the middle.

When Megan said this phrase during our conversation, I felt like she finally—finally!—put a title to what I had been feeling and, on some level, what had driven me to begin *Expectant Entrepreneur* in the first place: the feeling that I didn't belong. The flip side is the desire to seek out belongingness somewhere and with some community of women who knew what it meant to be exactly where I was in life.

After all, we *are* moms in the middle of two very clear identities: corporate mothers and stay-at-home mothers. But this weird middle means that many areas of our lives don't fit neatly or squarely into either identity. There are networking groups for business, and there are parenting groups for motherhood. But the merging of these two identities—business and motherhood—often doesn't happen without intention.

"Around the time I started using the phrase 'moms in the middle,' I was enrolled in an online business program," Megan said. "I had a four-month-old and a toddler at the time. One of the members of the business program commented within the group's Facebook page that she had just worked on her website for eight hours straight, and I immediately felt behind. How was I going to keep up with people

who had eight straight hours to focus on their business? I was essentially working with sprints of forty-five minutes while my kids napped, and there was a laundry list of things to tackle in those forty-five minutes."

That feeling of not belonging motivated Megan to start a subgroup specifically for mothers in the business program.

"I had felt really discouraged, and I knew there had to be other women feeling the same way," Megan said. "In fact, the woman who was leading this program, I knew for a fact she had children, but she never mentioned that fact, and so it made me feel like I shouldn't mention the fact that I have kids. But I did, and they impacted my experience. We needed to be talking about it—about how we can have kids and be in business and do them both really well."

Megan's experience is not dissimilar to my own experience with my first daughter. I was thirty when I had my first daughter Annie Jean, whom we affectionately call AJ.

One of my biggest blessings in life is that I have, like an avid hitchhiker collecting souvenirs on her journey, picked up the most amazing groups of friends and supporters throughout my life: friends from high school, college, and time living and working abroad in Spain, and friends who welcomed me into their groups when I found myself in need of friendship in Washington, DC, and Baltimore. I found friends who became like family, and friends I made through my husband and his family. I have business friends, networking groups, and people I can lean on when I need business advice. I had

friends who became moms before I did, and friends who became moms after me.

The day I turned thirty, my husband and I were sleeping in an extended-stay hotel while we were between living arrangements. We had sold our charming home in Norwood, Ohio, and were moving to a luxury apartment complex for the coming year so we could spend time searching for our next home. On my thirtieth birthday, I was also thirty-eight weeks pregnant. Whether it was the pregnancy hormones, the exhaustion from preparing and selling our home and moving, or the anticlimactic birthday dinner of Panera salads on a worn-out hotel room couch, I wept. I'll never forget the look on Adam's face as I sobbed into my baguette.

At that time, I couldn't articulate what I was feeling. In all honesty, I don't really think I could have identified what I was feeling even if I tried. In retrospect, it's clear to me: I was feeling desperately lonely. Not because I didn't feel loved by Adam or supported by him and my family and my friends. I was feeling lonely because I felt that no one *really* understood the position I was in. My network, despite all of the amazing people that I was (and continue to be) immensely grateful to have, was severely lacking other mother-entrepreneurs.

As I cried into my dinner that night, I was feeling very sorry for myself and incredibly anxious about how I was going to handle becoming a new mom and keeping my business—which was our family's only income, as my husband had left his job to be available as a stay-at-home dad—fully operational.

What I didn't realize at the time was that just days before, I had met some of the women who would turn out to be my community, my people. I had been invited to join a master-mind-style group of seven women entrepreneurs. But, I didn't know the role they would play in my life in the future. And on my birthday, I was craving someone, *anyone*, who could look me in the eye and tell me they understood what I was feeling and that I would truly believe they did.

This literal sob story is the moment in time that captures how deeply important community was for me, and I believe that this sentiment—this need to connect with other women who fundamentally relate to the identity of mother-entrepreneur—is one of the things that unites all of the women in this book, and so many of the women I've had the honor of meeting and incorporating into my network since I cried into a Panera dinner.

DISCOVERING THE MIDDLE

Earlier in this book, there's a surface-level introduction of the physical changes that pregnancy has on a woman's brain. There's also research that supports the fact that entrepreneurs' brains compute problems and solutions differently than those of non-entrepreneurs. These two explorations of the brain help to clarify, to some extent, the reason why I, personally, and many women interviewed for this book, felt a deep need to find and connect with other women like ourselves: we are, in fact, different than our non-entrepreneur mother friends, and we are, in fact, different than our non-mother entrepreneur friends.

There is a physiological component to who we are that distinguishes us from our peers, and when we layer in the emotions and experiences that are a result of this identity, my feeling so deeply drawn to find other women like me makes sense.

We have a human need to belong and experience intimate relationships. Motherhood, once we enter this phase of life, literally changes who we are. "The brain goes through all these changes when women are pregnant or postpartum—we call it 'pregnancy brain' or 'newborn stupidity'—but it's not stupid at all. It's the brain making sure the baby is first on the list, that the baby is the most fulfilling thing for now, because that is how the human race survives. We develop new aspects of ourselves that ever after are a part of who we are," clinical psychologist Laura Markham said.[36]

The importance of community in motherhood is a favorite topic of parenthood research and blogs. Passages like the one below by Anne-Marie Gambelin feel familiar to any mother who has researched the impact of motherhood—particularly new motherhood—on a woman.

"I knew I couldn't be the only woman who had given birth and was feeling this stranded: isolated, alone with my fears, lonely in my struggle to stay above water and desperate to look like I had things under control. The stress of it all pulled me down to depths I had never known before."[37]

36   Laura Markham, quoted in Rachel Bertsche, *The Kids Are in Bed: Finding Time for Yourself in the Chaos of Parenting* (New York: Penguin Press, 2020), 25.

37   Anne-Marie Gambelin, "I didn't expect the loneliness of new motherhood — or the importance of community," *Mother.ly* (blog), February

Rachel DesRochers, whose gratitude-based companies can be explored at her namesake website, remembers the innate need to find space in her role as mother to connect with other mothers.

"Community has been really important for me from as far back as I can remember, and something that has always been important to me in particular that I have space to share," Rachel said. "I knew I needed that space, so I started this mom's Breakfast Club. There was a breakfast potluck once a week, and we would either meet at somebody's house or at the park. And so that was my time every week that I knew I would be in community and my kids would be in community and I would have moms going through what I'm going through as a mom and we could just share together."

Similarly, the importance of community in entrepreneurship is widely accepted. "Entrepreneurship Is Inherently Lonely: The entire experience of creating and building a startup is filled with seeming contradictions. It's often thrilling yet nerve-wracking; it's filled with endless possibilities but also is incredibly risky; it surrounds you with a team of like-minded people, but it also is very lonely."[38]

The antidote to this loneliness, both in entrepreneurship and motherhood, is community. When I felt a lack of community, when that space between entrepreneurship and motherhood wasn't satisfied, I was left with an ongoing sense of longing—and an unrelenting desire to build that community in my life.

13, 2019.

38 Young Entrepreneurs Council, "Why Professional Networking is the Missing Piece to Your Success," Inc., February 22, 2018.

Formally, mother-entrepreneurs are building networks and communities to help satisfy this "middle." There are groups like Business Among Moms and the Founding Moms that seek out mother business owners, and thousands of groups targeted specifically at "mompreneurs."*

Anecdotally, mother-entrepreneurs are finding one another both virtually and in person to share their journeys and experiences. *Expectant Entrepreneur* captures the stories of a dozen or so women who were willing to tell their experiences for the sake of building this collection of shared stories.

THE EXPECTANT ENTREPRENEUR COMMUNITY

The next section of this book explores the stories of women who experienced their own unique journeys of motherhood and entrepreneurship. Some of the women I knew personally, and a handful of them have supported the *Expectant Entrepreneur* project since the first moment I shared it with them. Other women I reached out to randomly after reading an article they shared or seeing their name quoted in a piece, and they graciously accepted my invitation to participate in this book.

The process of my getting to know the women in this book varied with each woman, ranging from a single conversation with the intent of gathering anecdotes and hearing their stories for the first time to years of developing a friendship. Despite being located across the world, working in diverse industries, and managing companies of varying sizes, there are some remarkable similarities among us. Through their stories, I've come to better understand the experience of

these Expectant Entrepreneurs, who they are, and what this community of women shares.

The goal? Community. To fill the middle. To prevent other mother-entrepreneurs from crying over their Panera salads on the night of their thirtieth birthday because they felt disconnected from their amazing support groups. To be the new set of stories that reinforces that you—an expectant entrepreneur—have loads of experiences and characteristics in common with women across the world who understand exactly what you're feeling.

There's an entire cultural narrative that exists around the phrase "mompreneur" that could be an entire book on its own. Check out my personal take on the word in Chapter 3: Distinction Mompreneurs and Mother-Entrepreneurs.

7

Momentum

THE CHOICE TO MOVE FORWARD WITHOUT
UNDERSTANDING EXACTLY HOW.

Katie Garry knew she and her husband Ryan wanted a third child, and Katie was lucky in her ability to get pregnant without complications with her first two daughters. So when it came time to begin trying for their third child, momentum within her new business had a huge role in the conversation.

"I'm a year into my business, and it feels like things are really taking off," Katie said. At the time of our initial interview, Katie was only just beginning to explore what it would mean to have a baby during this season of her life. She had her first two daughters while working in a corporate environment. "I honestly tried to plan out everything perfectly so that I can have my next baby during the holidays so it doesn't impact the momentum of my business."

Katie launched her business, KG Creative, after she was laid off from her corporate job. But within a year, she had fully replaced, and then exceeded, her salary. The success of her

business in the first year was exciting, and she loved the new experience of being a business owner.

"It's hard though, because you work diligently to build up your clients and your work, and then you kind of get used to that cash flow and work flow," Katie said. "Ryan works full time, but we need my income, and that becomes even more important when you think about having another child. When we started talking about getting pregnant again, one of the first things I thought about was the impact it would have on my momentum as a business owner."

Momentum is the impetus gained by a moving object, and when it comes to motherhood and entrepreneurship, it is *everything*.

In motherhood, this forward energy begins well before you become a mom. For women like Leah Neaderthal, having a baby meant immense planning and preparation. She and her wife relied on in-vitro fertilization (IVF) and a donor to conceive their son, Noah.

"We wouldn't be able to be parents if we didn't plan in advance," Leah said. "We had to think through each step of the process, including multiple rounds of IVF, a miscarriage, and all of the financials that come with the process."

Leah's business, Smart Gets Paid, offers sales training to help women consultants and coaches land B2B clients. Leah's business thrives on an excellent sales funnel. Her success takes time, consistent marketing, expressing leadership to her clients, and sharing insights to gain traction with her

clients. In fact, her *entire* business is built around helping other women gain energy in *their* businesses, too.

"The momentum of my business was all I thought about," Leah shared. After becoming pregnant, Leah said she "dedicated the next nine months to prepping my business for maternity leave. I did this in a pretty methodical way. I hired five new team members. I set up systems. I 'processized' everything that could have a process. I knew I needed to maintain the drive in order to have a business once I returned from maternity leave."

Moms like Katie and Leah know that pregnancy creates a shockwave of energy and activity that impact a woman, her family situation, and her business. For me, the shockwave of energy and activity that came with the news I was expecting our second child was surprising, even though we knew another baby was on the horizon.

The moment I saw the positive pregnancy test, I was filled with excitement and relief and joy. And the moment right after that, I started to think and plan and consider my business. I crunched numbers to determine when my baby would be born, made assumptions about this pregnancy based on what I knew from my first, and immediately started outlining everything I wanted to do before the baby arrived.

Before spinning out of control, I remembered to share the news with my husband and decided not to make any major decisions until I had an official confirmation of the pregnancy with my doctor's office. But the energy and excitement that came with the news of a new baby quickly morphed

into a drive to move forward as the clock was ticking down to the due date.

And yet, even with all of our plans in place, things in both motherhood and business don't always go according to plan.

Rachel DesRochers, serial entrepreneur and owner of the company Grateful Grahams (among others), knows that even the best-laid plans can be thrown off course, and often right when you least expect it.

After trying for a baby for more than a year, Rachel finally found out she was pregnant. And then, within months, she was let go from her full-time marketing position.

"I had a newborn and no job," Rachel said. "A friend came over to visit me, and she brought a graham cracker cookie recipe with her. We baked together, and I was blown away by this recipe. Cooking and baking had always been a part of my life, and I really connected with the potential of this cookie. That was in January 2010. My husband I took $1,000 from our tax return that year and launched Grateful Grahams by April 1."

Momentum, in the case of many moms in the middle, is inspired by necessity. We run our businesses because we want to, but also because our families rely on us for income and stability. We wake up early to care for our children, then stay up late to care for our businesses. For better or for worse, momentum is essential to our experiences as business owners and as mothers.

"One of the traits of business owners that I grew up around and saw in my parents, and particularly my mom, is that it's hard to stop and can be a challenge to slow down," said Rachel Murphy, who grew up with entrepreneur parents and is now an owner of multiple businesses herself. "We create so much momentum that stopping is very hard to do, and while we might briefly slow down to absorb a situation, I find that mom business owners are particularly fast to move on to the next thing."

This energy we create and perpetuate is also the thing that is rocked to the core when we become pregnant. For some women, the physical impact of pregnancy is an initial threat to progress.

"Pregnancies are incredibly difficult for me," said Shawna Navaro, owner of Innerspace, a creative agency. "My body actually forces me to say no to a lot of things and slow down. I have to figure out how to get through each month, each day, and sometimes each hour. It's challenging."

Many mothers experience general fatigue during pregnancy, especially as we near the ninth month. For some mothers, the entire pregnancy is a forced period of time in which slowing down is a requirement.

A CLASSIC CASE OF CREATING MOMENTUM

Energy took on a new meaning for me in October 2019. I was eight months pregnant with Lena and feeling every bit of it. My husband just had shoulder surgery, and our daughter AJ was three and a half years old. I was running two businesses,

we were preparing for Lena's arrival, and we were heading into a wham-bam combination of newborn life and the holidays. I had two more business trips on the calendar, and one involved flying to Washington, DC, for a few days. In summary, we had a lot going on. The month prior to Adam's surgery, my anxiety was sky high.

How in the world am I going to handle all of this?

I tried to envision all the ways that things could go wrong, but then I shifted perspective to envision all the ways things could go right. Instead of worrying about how I was going to get things done, I just started getting things done. I looked into my business to find areas of progress I could double down on. I had a great team of freelancers, and I started to really let go of control and give my team the authority and independence they needed to move faster and more nimbly within Verano Marketing + Communications. We had drive as a team, and I loosened up my grip on all of the systems to see what would happen.

The more I let go, the faster we moved. The progress within my business allowed me to focus at home. I was in charge of getting AJ to and from day care until Adam got the approval to drive from his doctor. His surgery went exceptionally well, and my mother-in-law came to stay with us to help take care of him so I could keep moving in business, look after AJ, and find a little space for myself. My own mom stepped up, too, and among the three of us women, the energy was palpable. My mom helped me fully finish Lena's nursery and get her first year's worth of clothes into her bedroom so we didn't have to haul heavy items from the basement.

Adam liked to joke that we needed both of us to create 75 percent of a fully functioning adult. Between my pregnant body carrying forty extra pounds (yep) and his inability to lift anything or anyone, we had to find ways to make our lives easier before his surgery in October. We pulled holiday decor boxes up from the basement storage and had them ready to go in the dining room. We organized car seats, rearranged furniture, and assembled all the baby things we could think of. We cleaned and prepared and acted as if we were going to be stuck without help or assistance for weeks.

The reality is we didn't have to work this hard, as we are lucky to have an amazing group of family and friends who would do anything to help us if we needed it. But we did it, in part, because of momentum—a burst of energy before our household shifted into surgery-newborn-holiday-recovery era. I felt the pull to clear my head of household items that were on my to-do list and, once we did, I simply redirected that channel of energy right into my business.

For me, there was this short-term burst of commitment: a full-on sprint as we got closer to our family's "go time." But I had, in reality, been working all year to create the slow hum of business momentum. Scratch that: I had been working *for years* to create momentum in my business.

The first few years Verano was a business, I networked all day and worked in the evenings. I was growing my business during the time when "hustle," "boss bitch," and "slay all day" were trendy phrases. They spoke to my heart. I worked my tail off and, in retrospect, overworked myself. I don't recommend extreme overcommitment to work, but I have

to admit it moved my business forward. I built a network of people who liked and trusted me, and I took on projects of all shapes and sizes to start to understand what I did—and did not—like to do.

Work begets work for me, and one successful project consistently returned two or three referrals for more work. With time and consistency, my business grew over the first several years.

When my daughter AJ was born, energy looked different than it did when Lena was born. It was much more visceral with AJ. At that time, I had no contractors or 1099 workers supporting my business. It was all me, all the time. Then, success felt like a straight reflection of my hours worked. The more I worked, the more money I made. The energy stopped when I stopped, and it was scary to slow down. After AJ was born, I scheduled my first business meeting when she was four weeks old, and I brought her with me. Downtime meant a downturn in business.

To try to bridge the gap of time I was going to be out of the office, Adam and I hired a college student to help support the business. The co-op, Lindsey, was great, and she did very well with the work we handed to her. Adam took over some email and financial responsibilities, and they nurtured new leads as best as they could.

Momentum, at that time, meant doing as much work as possible until I couldn't work anymore. I wrote articles in advance, asked clients for a list of as many deliverables as they could think of that I could work on in advance of my

"maternity leave," and I worked long days and nights to get as much completed as possible before AJ was born. This preparation felt like the right choice for me at the time, primarily because it was the only way I thought Verano would survive.

Verano did survive, and just a few months after AJ was born, we secured a yearlong contract that remains my largest contract to date. With Lena, momentum meant letting go and bringing in as many people as I could afford to allow more energy, more ideas, and more work to flow among us. I planned to step back and not be the funnel for all work and all communication. I introduced team members, and I let go of the need to oversee every aspect of the business. I tried to observe and understand where energy existed in business and my personal life, and I grabbed onto it dearly.

Adam's surgery was a success. My daughter was born a week early, healthy and strong. We had the holidays exactly as planned, and business marched forward. Momentum carried us, as a family, and Verano, as a business, during an incredibly challenging season of life, and yet we came out smiling and healthy on the other side.

The thoughts around progress churn for Expectant Entrepreneurs. We work to build energy in our businesses before, during, and after pregnancies. During the months leading up to the birth of our children, we look to all the areas of our businesses to establish momentum and keep new business coming in and successful projects being returned to clients. We evaluate our sales cycles and processes to ensure everyone has what they need to keep moving forward.

At home, we use our energy and systems to plan, prepare, and survive, especially if we have other children to care for at the same time. We learn to listen to our bodies, and when we get waves of functional energy—watch out! We will get as much done as we can, cherishing those moments of feeling well to spend time with our children, prepare for the baby, and care for ourselves as much as possible.

We learn that momentum can be borrowed, shared, and contagious.

8

Curiosity

In his famous book *Start with Why: How Great Leaders
Inspire Everyone to Take Action*, Simon Sinek leads his read-
ers through his journey about finding the "why" of your business or your purpose. The idea and positioning is incredibly
compelling, and nearly every working professional I've come
across over the past decade is familiar with the concept. In
fact, Sinek's TED Talk on the subject has been viewed more
than 28 million times—the third most popular TED video
of all time.[39]

The idea of starting with why, from Sinek's perspective, is
about defining "a deep-seated purpose, cause, or belief that
is the source of our passion and inspiration."[40] It's an internal search, whether that's a look inside yourself to discover

---

39   Simon Sinek, "How Great Leaders Inspire Action," Filmed September
     2009 at TEDxPuget Sound, Puget Sound, WA.
40   Ibid.

your personal why or a deeper look into your business for an organizational why.

It's an important question, and every entrepreneur and business owner is likely familiar with their own business' why: What drives us to do what we do? Why, truly, do we take this road, which is arguably less smooth and a bit bumpier than a more traditional professional path? The why tells the purpose for which we live and run our businesses—the thing that makes it all worthwhile.

In the world of entrepreneurism and parenting, there's a second type of why question: the why of curiosity and, in both areas of life, a persistent ability to ask ourselves and others why again and again and again.

Why do we do it this way?

Why is this working?

Why isn't this working?

Why do I love this product?

Why do my kids love this?

Why isn't there an easier way to do this?

Why are we still doing it like this?

Why hasn't someone come up with a new way?

Why do I care about this?

Why do I bother?

My personal favorite is "Why am I so tired?," but I think we all know the answer to that. Truly, behind every great business, there's a great why. I also believe behind every great family there's a compelling why. A hallmark characteristic of an Expectant Entrepreneur is the ability to question things again and again and be okay with not having a solution right away. Entrepreneurs and mothers are both able to embrace varying perspectives in an effort to see things differently, explore new solutions, and figure out what works best for them.

"The fact that I was coming at it from a totally different angle—a mom angle, frankly—is what allowed me to ask questions," said Kate Torgersen, founder of Milk Stork, during IDEO's Creative Confidence webinar.[41] "Why does it have to be this way, or why can't we do it this way? I wasn't entrenched in anything. So, it gave me a lot of freedom to challenge. I had a lot of people say like, you can't do it that way, and I asked why."

This pushback Kate experienced is normal, according to Thomas Fogarty, a surgeon at Stanford University Medical Center who invented the first balloon catheter to be used therapeutically. There's a perception that going against the grain and pushing for a better solution is about ego. "Getting

---

41   Kate Torgerson, "What Motherhood Taught this CEO About Starting a Business," Interview by IDEO, May 6, 2020.

people to expand their views—to see a situation through others' eyes—often raises ego issues. People don't want to believe that they're doing things in ways that are less than optimal. In fact, one of the hardest things about innovation is getting people to accept that the way they work just might not be the best."[42]

The power of why, from this perspective, is less about ego and more about curiosity: *why is this the way?*

After Mother's Day 2020, I opened up my business notebook to where I put my daily thought downloads and make my to-do list for the day. The page that would have been Monday was marked up with my three-year-old's doodles and scratches. She had asked me over the weekend to show her which "ABCs" make the word "Mom." She had been practicing writing out "mom" for the card she was creating for me, and the evidence was scribbled all over my notebook.

Over and over on the page, there were shapes that clearly represented o's (easy!) and other humps and loops and lines that only very vaguely represented m's. I remember the exchange we had as she practiced her letters.

AJ: Mama, how do you write "mom"?

Me: Like this: M-O-M. Mom!

AJ: Why do we write it that way?

---

42 Thomas Fogarty quoted in "Inspiring Innovation," *Harvard Business Review,* August 2002.

Me: Well, those are the letters that make the sounds for the word "mom."

AJ: Okay. But why does an M look like that?

Me: Actually, I'm not sure. But, it just does. That's how we learn to make the sounds of letters so we can read them.

AJ: But WHY does an M have two humps, and an N has one? And WHY does an O look like a zero? Is an O a zero?

Me: Well, I don't know. That's a great question. Let's ask Miss Emily about that next week.

At that point, I bailed on the conversation and diverted to AJ's preschool teacher, Miss Emily, who was hosting twice-a-week Zoom calls for AJ's preschool class while the school was closed for the COVID-19 pandemic. *As a side note, I'm incredibly grateful to teachers, before, during, and after COVID-19.*

But AJ's curiosity struck a chord in me. She wanted to know *why* she had to learn it this way. Who made the rules? How did we get to this conclusion?

The truth is, there are hundreds of things we do every day that are simply part of life because that's what we learned. This acceptance is evolutionary, in a lot of ways. There are numerous studies that examine herd mentality from a negative perspective that specifically call out a lack of critical thinking; however, from a busy mother-entrepreneur's perspective, herd mentality is essential in some aspects of life.

Simply put, there's not enough time in a day to critically think about every decision. If we spend all our time examining the potential solutions or products and all of their competitors, we would simply run out of brain ammunition and time. This is where good marketing and online reviews will win business:

"Popularity is seen as an indication of better quality, and consumers will use the opinions of others posted on these platforms as a powerful compass to guide them towards products and brands that align with their preconceptions and the decisions of others in their peer groups."[43]

At the heart of innovation, someone, somewhere asked the right why at the right time. Why don't women have a better travel solution for breast milk? Why can't we do this a different way?

Kate Torgersen's frustration as a working mom who wanted to feed her children while she traveled fueled her development as an entrepreneur. An article from Warren Berger on Success.com gets to the power of inquiry. Curiosity, or inquiry, can lead to:

- More productivity: Studies have found that people are likely to do more of a task if they pose it as a question. For instance: "I need to write more for my book," yields to fewer results than the question, "How can I write more for my book?"

---

43   C. Whan Park and V. Parker Lessig, "Students and Housewives: Differences in Susceptibility to Reference Group Influence," *Journal of Consumer Research*, no 2 (1977): 102.

- More solutions: In his research, Berger found that most innovators and entrepreneurs developed their solutions by first asking a series of questions, like, "Why is this a problem?," followed by, "How might I do this differently?"
- More business success: Hal Gregersen studied the success of high-profile leaders and found that asking questions over and over helped to "turbocharge" their success by developing new ways to lead companies and new systems that better served their teams.
- More personal clarity: Berger noted that most entrepreneurs he talked with had a high ability to self-question to discover their path, such as, "Am I on the right path? What fulfills me as a person?"
- Better adaptation: By asking questions and being curious, we're better able to take information, process it, and think about how we might add to it ourselves, resulting in better adaptation and adjustment in a rapidly changing society.[44]

As my daughter pointed out to me, there are plenty of questions we can ask—and she asks a LOT of them all the time. Parents have the particular luxury of being the guardians of all the answers for their children, at least for a few years in life. AJ asks Adam and me questions all the time because she believes we have all the answers. And she doesn't think less of us when we say we don't know—in fact, she often challenges us to come up with our own answers anyway.

"But Mom, WHY do ABCs look this way?"

---

44 Warren Berger, "Question Everything," *Success*, May 16, 2014.

"AJ, honey, I really don't know why these are the shapes of the letters."

"Well, just make something up! It's okay. Just tell me why."

I don't recall exactly what my answer was, but it seemed to either satisfy her curiosity or be so off-putting that she quit asking me questions. One way or another, she reminded me that asking questions is natural, and children are the best example of this. They are curious all the time, and for many moms, to the point of exhaustion. They remind us that it's okay to try to understand the world around you and to not accept the most popular solution as the only one.

"We get to choose," said Rachel Murphy, life coach and owner of Mindsettings. "As business owners and moms, we're constantly scanning our peers and our clients and our neighbors and friends to see what's working for them. We learn that what's working for one business or one family doesn't have to be the way it's going to work for me, and we take those lessons and apply them everywhere. We get to choose when bedtime works best for our family or if our kids get to pick out their own clothes. In business, when I see somebody else have success, we get to choose what that means to us. Maybe it inspires us to try something new, or maybe we borrow their ideas for our own businesses. We get to observe, and we get to choose."

We ask questions, and we choose what works best for our families and our businesses. The curiosity of our children reminds us to ask the questions, explore everything, and be patient as they explore big, big worlds that open up to

them. As business owners, we are the decision-makers: we get to ask the questions, explore everything, and be patient with ourselves and our success as we learn how to make things better and improve our world around us. As Expectant Entrepreneurs, our desire for things to be different and for our lives to meet expectations drives efficiencies, solutions, risks, and innovations.

Curiosity wakes the creators.

9

Empathy

THE ABILITY TO REMAIN ATTUNED TO THE
EMOTIONS AND NEEDS OF OTHERS, NAMELY
OUR CHILDREN AND OUR CLIENTS.

Wednesdays are for collaboration. At least this is the rule for Clair Jones and Caroline Maurer. As mentioned earlier in this book, Clair and Caroline are the co-owners of Witty Kitty Digital, a business they've owned together for years, working remotely from Salt Lake City and Portland, Maine. When they both became mothers within six months, planning and time blocking became essential—as did empathy.

"The biggest struggle is scheduling," Clair said. "We have it worked out to offer some balance to each of us, and we're very lucky that we co-founded this business together and are going through similar life phases. And, on top of that, we work with a lot of women business owners, and we love working with them because they're a bit more understanding of what we're going through."

On Wednesdays, Clair and Caroline agreed to both be active within their business. The other days? They tried to do as much planning as possible and then being flexible with the rest.

"We just know that if one of us is having a bad day, the other one steps up and can pick up some of the slack so it doesn't pile up," Clair said.

This understanding is empathy, and our ability to be empathetic to another person's situation grows and changes as we birth and raise our children. A great business partner certainly doesn't have to be a fellow woman or a fellow parent. Gender and parenting status are not prerequisites for showing empathy to your colleagues or clients, and there are countless examples of amazing people being kind, generous, and empathic without also being a mother or an entrepreneur.

But, in the case of Clair and Caroline, they were helped by their shared understanding of what a fellow mom and business owner is experiencing. The study from Nature Neuroscience, referenced earlier in this book, found that the hormonal changes that started in pregnancy persisted even two years after pregnancy, confirming lasting impacts of hormone surges on a woman's brain.

"...[Even] two years after pregnancy, women had gray matter brain changes in regions involved in social cognition or the

ability to empathically understand what is going on in the mind of another person, to put yourself in their shoes."[45]

Getting into the mind of another person and tapping into the ability to recognize emotions and empathize with another's situation are essential elements of both parenting and entrepreneurship.

"Yes, our brains are impacted during pregnancy," Megan Flatt said. "But what I think this translates to is that we are more emotionally connected to our clients, too. We're more emotionally connected to our team members. We're generally more empathetic, because from a biological standpoint, we've developed these skills."

Motherhood makes us this way. Entrepreneurship and client service encourage us to flex it.

Showing empathy in business is a superpower of great leaders and, arguably, great marketers. How better to connect with your audience than to tap into what they're feeling, how they're interpreting your messaging, and how they might use the service or products you're offering them?

"Empathizing allows the entrepreneur to understand what motivates his consumer and gives him a glimpse into what the consumer really wants. I say really wants because most

---

45 Elaine Hoekzema et al, "Pregnancy leads to long-lasting changes in human brain structure," *Nature Neuroscience 20*, no 2 (February 2017): 287-296.

of the time the consumer has no clue as to what they really want."[46]

As entrepreneurs, we're often highly involved in the way our business is marketed and portrayed publicly, and for many small businesses, our identities are deeply connected to the businesses and brands we promote. On the flip side, a lack of empathy and understanding can be the downfall of a business, and Marie Englesson knows this experience personally.

After running a business in Tanzania for six years, Marie was excited to learn that she was expecting her first baby—a son. She anticipated that being an Expectant Entrepreneur would force some business issues to rise to the surface, but she didn't exactly foresee how the events would unfold.

"Because I was in a place where hospitals were not great, giving birth would mean that I would have to be away for quite a long time," Marie said. "I would be gone from the business for at least six months, and maybe more."

Marie knew she would have to step back as CEO during her transition to motherhood. In doing so, there would be financial implications for her beauty store business, which had multiple brick-and-mortar locations across the country.

"I had been taking a low salary for the health of the business, but that would need to change if we hired someone on to take my place," Marie said. "That would cost quite a bit more,

---

46 Paul Hudson, "Why the Most Successful Entrepreneurs are the Least Egotistical," *EliteDaily*, September 13, 2013.

so I knew we needed to have investors if the business was going to survive."

In the business environment in Tanzania, Marie reached out to primarily men investors outside of her business for funding.

"All of the investors I approached told me to reach back out for funds when I was back in the business after my baby was born, which obviously wasn't going to work," Marie said. "And in my experience, investors always tell me that they invest in the entrepreneurs, and if the entrepreneur is not fully committed, it's really a red flag for them."

As a Swedish citizen, Marie was entitled to eighteen months of paid maternity leave, and she was planning to take advantage of that country's maternity support by returning to Sweden to birth and raise her son for the first eighteen months of his life.

"In the end, it worked out," Marie said. "I knew either I needed to scale up the business or get out of it at that point, and the pregnancy turned out to give me a bit of an exit plan."

Marie decided to sell her business after the financing round she was pursuing failed. The lack of funding—and the unwillingness to invest in a pregnant woman—would have been an unfortunate end to a business' story.

Thankfully, Marie's story isn't a sad one. Everything worked out well for Marie, who safely gave birth to her son in Sweden and stayed with family before returning to Africa to be with

her husband. He came to visit for the birth and returned to his work in Africa after a couple of weeks.

Marie's business is still in operations under the new owners, and her team is running the business to this day, nearly two and a half years later.

"As I left, the team I built really stepped up," Marie said. "Sometimes, others have the chance to grow if you step aside—and that was actually what happened when I left."

While Marie's path and her business' path have both continued on with success, many women do not have the same backup plan and national benefits.

Interestingly, empathy can—and is—being taught for the purposes of building better businesses. In *The Role of Empathy in Entrepreneurship: A Core Competency of the Entrepreneurial Mindset*, the authors explain the critical link between empathy and successful entrepreneurs:

"A common goal of entrepreneurship education is developing an entrepreneurial mindset in students. Furthermore, a key competency of an entrepreneurial mindset is the ability to empathize with others. Empathy is a cognitive and affective process fostering the capability of understanding and appreciating the feelings, thoughts, and experiences of others. Since entrepreneurship is about introducing innovations into a community, having a keen understanding and

appreciation of the needs and desires of community members is an important entrepreneurial skill."[47]

In their research, the authors note that one of the most convincing benefits of empathy in successful entrepreneurs is that it enables us to reduce the negative effects of cognitive bias. In other words, we're better able to see the world from multiple perspectives (think: children, for instance, or customers facing a challenge) and not quickly assume they interpret the world around them in the same way as we do—and we seek to work and partner with people who are able to be empathetic, too.

Like Marie's story, the loss of some business was not necessarily a negative, as it reflects a discord in values that are important to business owners as we build our companies.

Genna Gardner, owner of a digital marketing firm in Cincinnati, was just beginning to grow her business when she found out she was pregnant with her third son.

"I thought, for just a moment, that pregnancy might be a reason I would lose business," Genna said. "But then, just as fast, I realized I wouldn't want to work with someone who didn't want to work with a mother of three boys."

On a larger scale, empathy may also be the reason we witness more community giveback and development by women executives over their men counterparts. According to a Forbes

47   Russel Korte et al, "The Role of Empathy in Entrepreneurship: A Core Competency of the Entrepreneurial Mindset," *Advances in Engineering Education* 7, no. 1 (2018): n1.

article, women are more likely to prioritize corporate social responsibility over their men counterparts:

"Mounds of data indicate that female-led companies are more likely to prioritize corporate social responsibility initiatives. Research by Kellie McElhaney, the founder of the Center for Gender Equity & Leadership at the University of California at Berkeley's Haas School of Business, has found that companies that have women on their corporate boards are more focused on environmental, social, and governance issues than companies with no female board members."[48]

From a human-centered approach, Decety and Jackson described empathy as developing a sense of similar, but separate, feelings of others.[49] In its various forms, empathy includes caring for others, experiencing the emotions of others, and discerning what others feel and think. Broader definitions include more distant stakeholders (in time and space) and non-human entities, such as the environment or ecosystem.[50]

Expectant Entrepreneurs are better equipped with empathy tools, which are then sharpened and refocused during business growth—and the more we use those tools, the more able

---

48   Falon Fatemi, "The Value of Investing in Female Founders," *Forbes,* March 29, 2019.

49   Jean Decety and Philip L. Jackson, "The functional architecture of human empathy," *Behavioral and cognitive neuroscience reviews* 3, no. 2 (2004): 71-100.

50   Russel Korte et al. "The Role of Empathy in Entrepreneurship: A Core Competency of the Entrepreneurial Mindset." *Advances in Engineering Education* 7, no. 1 (2018): n1.

we are to put them into play in our businesses and families again and again.

Just as Clair and Caroline used their empathy to better build an effective schedule, and Marie found a lack of empathy as a clean exit strategy for her business, Expectant Entrepreneurs are able to identify the needs of others to create more fulfilling, effective businesses and more nurturing families.

Empathy, as it turns out, is a superpower of both entrepreneurs and mothers, and our lives as mother-business owners consistently reinforces and strengthens our empathetic prowess.

10

Big-Picture Thinking

**THE ABILITY TO SEE THE POTENTIAL
OF YOUR FUTURE.**

My husband and I call the first few months at home with a new baby "one hundred days of darkness." It's our attempt to make light of those first weeks of sleeplessness, newborn cries, breastfeeding trial and error, and my bodily pains. There's nothing quite like the overwhelming sense of a new little human who is fully and completely dependent upon you for everything.

But, we survived it, and three years later, we decided to face those days again. We opted in to one hundred days of darkness with full awareness of the challenges of caring for a newborn baby because we saw a bigger picture for our family. We saw past the two-hour round-the-clock feedings, the laptop-sized sanitary pads, and the hefty hospital bills because we knew we were meant for more as parents.

In the same way, entrepreneurs have the same tension between the short-term reality and the long-term possibilities.

We take on the debt, leave stable jobs, learn new skills, and take the risk of failure because of what *could be*. We're hard-pressed to leave opportunities and potential on the table. We grind through the first few years *because* we know the next few years will reap the benefits. Even on the days when the phone won't stop ringing or emails seem to replenish by the minute, there's a vision.

When we can't see past our noses because we're buried in daily tasks and to-do lists, somewhere in our minds, there's a small, ever-present nugget of a vision of what our futures could be if we just keep going.

"When my husband and I moved back to Finland, I had left my job and found myself in the middle of the suburbs of Helsinki," said Maria Friström, owner of Hem Essen Oy/Home Aces Ltd., a real estate development company. "My first son was eight months old, and I was four months pregnant with my second. I didn't have a network of business professionals. But my thought was okay—that's okay. I'll start from scratch."

Maria saw the big picture of what her business idea could become in Finland. She saw an opportunity to break the trend in her local real estate market.

"One of the things I noticed when we first moved here is that I had a really hard time finding an apartment that I loved," she said. "I found so many nice ones, but the style was very rigid. All whites and grays and very similar. There was no color, no true design."

So with an eight-month-old in tow and a baby on the way, she launched her real estate development company. As an Expectant Entrepreneur, Maria didn't focus on the challenges of her current reality. She saw an opportunity to create something bigger for herself and, in turn, for the family she and her husband were growing.

Expectant Entrepreneurs don't always give ourselves time to fully daydream about the big picture. A common theme throughout many of these women's stories is that while we all know that we are working toward *something else*, we can't always see what the something else truly is. But there's a quiet curiosity that remains, even when it's muffled by the daily focus on calendars and schedules and the here and now.

"When I really stop to think about things, being a mom is really all about pushing through," said Rachel DesRochers, owner of Grateful Grahams. "We are creating our own guidebook for how to be a mom. Every day is white space—sometimes every minute is white space—that we get to fill in."

"I know that I am okay with being a little scared. I think most moms are. It's really scary when you hold your kid for the first time and realize that you are going to guide them for at least the next eighteen years and be very involved and know as much about them as possible to help them become who they are supposed to be. Starting a business is a lot like that."

The ability to be scared, take risks, and persevere is part of the ability to see the big picture. We wouldn't be scared if we could see the clear path ahead of us. We wouldn't take risks

if we didn't think more was possible. We wouldn't persevere if there weren't a reason to keep pushing on.

Big-picture thinking often disguises itself in the form of daily business decisions and household conversations. The difference is that Expectant Entrepreneurs are willing to be uncomfortable, get a little scared, assume the financial responsibilities, open the companies, have the children, and move forward every day because we believe we can create a future for ourselves that's worth the daily effort.

We don't want to leave potential untapped. We want to *try*. We're not just daydreamers and visionaries. We're those things *and* we execute what needs to happen to bring them to fruition. The big picture is often hidden in sacrifices and hits to our egos, yet we move forward because we believe that more is possible if we continue to explore.

For Dawn Schwartzman, her bigger picture developed over time. In 1982, Dawn and her then-husband launched Enriching Spaces, a dealership that specializes in furnishings, interior design, and project management for inspired workspaces. She became an entrepreneur in an era when women-owned businesses were significantly less common in the United States than they are today.

"In the early years, it felt important that [my husband] had the title of president," Dawn said. "I don't remember my title then. In our industry, men held most of the leadership and sales positions. I spent my time filling in all of the gaps at work—making sure projects were moving forward and everyone had what they needed to sell and generate business, and

I would handle everything behind the scenes. Then I would go home and do the exact same thing: make sure my kids had everything they needed."

Today, Dawn is the sole owner of Enriching Spaces. She saw the importance of the big picture while the business was growing. The vision expanded to include more human-centered design with a focus on health and wellness. She was adaptable to slipping in and out of roles to help the company reach its potential.

"I believe that it was important then for my children, and now with my grandkids, to show them how and what's possible," Dawn said. "You can have a career or own a business and raise a family. Most of my friends are retired, but I am grateful for the ongoing opportunity to learn, grow, and design the work that I have passion for."

Whether it's for next-generation inspiration or a desire to push our own potential to its max capacity, seeing the big picture is essential for Expectant Entrepreneurs. We finish the tasks, create the schedules, and do the daily things not because we have to, but because we believe in the challenge of expecting more from ourselves and our lives.

We're not just daydreamers and visionaries. We're big-picture thinkers who know how to dream without losing sight of what has to happen—sometimes down to the minute—to make our futures possible.

11

Creativity

Creativity, by definition, is the ability to imagine. Entrepreneurs are known for our ability to put aside the reality of what's in front of us, like resources, materials, problems, existing platforms, and known solutions, and envision something new. When expressed aloud, creativity sounds like "what if" and "have we considered" or "could this work?" In our minds, it's a million little pieces of the puzzle being disassembled, rearranged, deconstructed, reimagined, and then executed with strategy and intention.

Creativity doesn't always take glamorous forms. Sometimes, creativity is required to simply get to a system that functions. Both parenthood and entrepreneurship are ripe with creativity in large, overt ways and small, simple daily wins. Creativity can be large and impressive, like pivoting your business in the time of a global pandemic. It can also be quiet

and subtle, like finding quick ways to entertain a child if you need to take a last-minute conference call at home.

In anticipation of the arrival of her third child, Katie Garry, owner of KG Creative, built out the systems and procedures in her business and her household—not out of a need for structure and organization, but for want of creativity.

"Having systems or spaces for things and ideas gives my brain the rigidity of structure," Katie said. "But then, because I have a defined structure to start from, I have the freedom and brain space to think creatively about problems. It helps me be more creative and flexible. I need the box, but then I want to break the box."

Katie isn't alone in her approach. Developing systems helps creativity flourish in functional ways. Structure helps creative people bridge the gap from ideation and big-picture thinking to practical application.

"An entrepreneur provides the 'science' aspect about how to bring the artistic creativity to life. Therefore, an entrepreneur bridges the gap between the creative genius and a traditional business approach."[51]

Innovation and creativity are naturally popular topics in the worlds of both entrepreneurship and parenthood. Entrepreneurial websites are littered with the importance of the creativity in business, articles on how to become more creative,

---

51 Kyung Hee Kim, "The Creativity Crisis: The Decrease in Creative Thinking Scores on the Torrance Tests of Creative Thinking," *Creativity Research Journal* 23, no. 4 (October 1, 2011): 285–95.

quick tips to thinking more creatively, and more. Similarly, any quick look at blogs and websites targeted at mothers of young children will have creativity written all over them:

- Creative Living With Kids
- Creative Kid Snacks
- Eco-Friendly Crafts
- The Growing Creatives
- Creative Kids
- Creativity for Kids

These activities are popular because kids are filled with imagination, and they love to express their creativity. They haven't yet learned the confines of societal, familial, and cultural expectations. Their brains create stories that are fun and exciting adventures through the bits and pieces of the world they've experienced.

"Children and adults depend on their creative abilities to help them adapt and thrive in increasingly complex and uncertain times," wrote Marilyn Price-Mitchell, PhD, founder of Roots of Action. "Researchers believe that a creative life fosters happiness and wellbeing, and that there is a significant connection between creativity, meaning, and intrinsic motivation."[52]

Leah Neaderthal, owner of Smart Gets Paid, took her ability to problem-solve to the next level, pairing her creativity with her goal of developing processes and streamlining. After having her son Noah, Leah realized that things she knew

---

52   Marilyn Price Mitchell, Ph.D., "Creativity: How Parents Nurture the Evolution of Children's Ideas," *Roots of Action (blog)*, April 10, 2017.

about her baby were incredibly helpful in solving problems throughout the day. For instance, Noah had several different types of cries, but not all people who hear a baby's cries will be able to distinguish differences among them. Leah also knew her son's schedule and preferences, both of which are things she learned over time. Family members, nannies, and other people who would potentially be stepping in to care for Noah wouldn't have the firsthand experiences to draw from to be able to calm Noah and provide him with what he needed, be it a bottle, fresh diaper, a nap, or entertainment.

The creative solution? She developed a flowchart with a decision tree showing exactly how to figure out what Noah wants and what steps to take next.

The connections among creativity and parenthood and entrepreneurship are notable: in the United States, students' creative thinking scores decrease significantly from kindergarten through third grade, then remain static or decrease starting in sixth grade. Yet the very definition of an entrepreneur is someone who has enough creativity to see a new business concept, model, or service in the existing marketplace.

Entrepreneurship "is often driven by the vision of the founder(s) who believe they can solve a problem in a smarter, better, more efficient way than anyone else currently on the market," said Ron Ben-Zeev, founder and CEO of World Housing Solution. "That ability to visualize then develop and implement

the solution is what fuels those who launch and run companies. It's the driving force behind their creativity."[53]

In that way, entrepreneurs are adults who have managed to retain their ability to incorporate innovation and creative problem solving into their everyday world. And, as mothers, we're surrounded by our children's natural tendencies toward creativity and imagination.

There's a beautiful, cyclical nature to the relationship between Expectant Entrepreneurs and creativity: creative children grow into creative adults who launch creative businesses, reinforcing creativity in the next generation.

---

53 "How to Harness Creativity as an Entrepreneur," *Start Your Business (blog), Business News Daily,* March 5, 2020.

12

Flexibility

WHAT IS LIFE WITH KIDS WITHOUT FLEXIBILITY? WHO IS AN ENTREPRENEUR WITHOUT THE ABILITY TO CHANGE?

One of the most reassuring messages I heard from other moms is that everything changes all the time. From the very beginning of our baby's lives, there's a cycle of learning what your baby wants and needs, mastering that phase, and then right when you've found your rhythm and you take a deep sigh of relief, everything changes.

Hearing this story from other mothers made me feel better. There is no magic method of mastering my child's schedule. The best plan is to be relatively plan-less, help my baby thrive in this phase, then get ready to do it all over again. In fact, an indicator of children thriving is change. Pediatricians will check to ensure they're changing: Are they putting on weight? Trying new sounds? Reaching for people they love? Babies grow, reach new milestones, learn new skills, and demand different routines and types of care. As parents, we learn to be flexible because we know change is critical to success.

Business requires change and flexibility, too. Just like a child, a business doesn't come out of the gate fully functioning and independent. There are systems that need to be developed, lessons to be learned, marketing to try, and customers to nurture. When I was in my fourth year of business and my first daughter was a year old, I lost an enormous client for a few important reasons, many of which were totally rational and had nothing to do with work performance. There were a lot of tears and so much fear about how I was going to be able to rebound in my business quickly enough to not put our home and assets on the line.

I learned a huge lesson about letting one client take too much control over my business. I needed to be flexible more than ever. That client was gone, and I needed to rebound. Flexibility was critical in my ability to do so, and it took me six months to feel like I was on sure footing again, but I learned what I needed to learn and walked away a much stronger business.

Mothers and entrepreneurs both need to be flexible in their daily lives as well as with the "big picture." In addition to being flexible with the direction of your business after a big loss, there are small, seemingly insignificant flexes that happen every day. When a kid gets sick, we quickly pivot and change our plans for the day. When a client offers feedback on a project that requires a shift, we respond with adjustments and new ideas.

"Every four months or so, there's a huge learning curve for me," said Shawna Navaro, owner of Innerspace, a creative design studio. "I've just realized over time that in both

business and at home, our schedule changes pretty dramatically a few times a year. We're constantly juggling how to make everything fit, and finally my husband and I realized we don't need to find what's going to work for years and years. We just need to find what will for right now."

There are *some* limits to flexibility, and that's where boundaries come into play. Boundaries are another aspect of what it takes to be an Expectant Entrepreneur. With opinions and insights from many well-intentioned people on parenting styles and business decisions, determining when to be flexible can be a challenge. Business owners and parents both learn with time that boundaries are particularly important for sanity and progress. Flexibility has limits.

"Boundaries are a big discussion," said Nana Moore, who runs a community for business-owning mothers as well as her own digital operations consulting business, the Ops Collective. "If you don't set them up, you become too flexible and people take advantage."

Boundaries for our own productivity, time, and schedule requirements are also directly connected to flexibility. Between children's changing schedules and client demands, retaining a level of malleability is essential. But bending too far by overworking, packing schedules, and being at every child's school event can result in stress, reduced productivity, and declines in mental and physical health.

"One of the things I constantly need to remind myself of is that I'm in charge of managing how much I take on, and when I'm taking things on," said Genna Gardner, owner of

Elevate Digital. "This is one of the benefits of being a business owner during pregnancy—there's a lot of flexibility in determining what stays and what goes."

Expectant Entrepreneurs must find ways to be flexible within their days, and flexible in how they grow their business and their families. We risk achieving the full potential of our businesses, and we stifle the growth of our children and families if we don't allow for change. Without the capacity to react to new feedback and information, we remain stuck where we are.

Flexibility feeds into resilience, persistence, momentum, big-picture thinking, and so many other aspects of what it means to be an Expectant Entrepreneur. In order to achieve the big picture we see for ourselves, we need to be open to the many ways of *how* we get there. In order to maintain momentum, we need to respond to setbacks or challenges with creativity. In order to get back up after we feel knocked down, we must be agile in our view of failures and successes.

There is an art to finding your personal sweet spot between remaining flexible and upholding boundaries. Expectant Entrepreneurs are particularly adept at finding our limits and sticking with them, but only after practice and refinement over many years and experiences.

13

Focus

"Managing a household with four children as a single mom is like running a business. It feels very much one in the same. Every day, you have to make sure everything is taken care of. Did I get the appointments? Did I check all of the lists? Being a mother of a larger family prepared me to be a business owner. I can change direction of my focus in a moment's notice. I work on little sleep, and I work until the job is complete. We don't waiver in the face of setbacks. When there are days that I work hard and long and I'm tired, I know I'm modeling and displaying what hard work looks like. I'll never apologize for that."

Nikki Laub, owner of Premiere Concrete Supply, in many ways, works in a "man's world." She has four sons and works in the commercial construction world. She knows that her business' performance is under a fraction more scrutiny than her competitors', specifically because she's a woman working in a historically man-dominated industry. But being a single mother of four boys keeps her focused on her mission:

showing her sons that while she might need a little extra energy and focus some days, women can run successful businesses in *any* industry if they choose to.

Expectant Entrepreneurs are the C-suite executives of our own businesses. We often assume multiple roles within our businesses, particularly as they grow. From sales to customer service to execution of work, we've likely done every task within our companies at some point. We have people who rely on our business for their own financial well-being, and we have our own family's financial well-being on our resume. Simultaneously, many Expectant Entrepreneurs begin their businesses as a way to control their time and schedule. Ideally, when children enter the picture, we use this ability to control our calendars as a way to be present, involved mothers. Time feels fleeting, and fleeting feels generous.

Every person has the same amount of time in a day—twenty-four hours—and you use them however you want. When you run a business and you're growing a family, twenty-four hours feels like five minutes, and there never seems to be enough.

"I try to ask myself the question of nine. Will this matter in nine minutes, nine hours, nine days, nine weeks, nine months or nine years? If it will truly matter for all of those, pay attention to it. If it isn't going to matter in nine minutes, nine hours or nine days from now, you need to not pay attention to it," wrote Whitney Wolf Herd, founder and CEO of Bumble, a social and dating app, and a cofounder

of the dating app Tinder, in an *Entrepreneur* article.[54] "This concept of nine has kept me on track from losing focus on the things that truly matter. That way you can respond when you need to, but you don't spend your time reacting to things that are not going to have any importance in a short period of time from now."

The ability to focus and execute ideas is a hallmark of entrepreneurs. It's been cited as the number one indicator of business success in entrepreneurs.[55] The reason is that focus serves as the bridge between creativity and big-picture ideas and between execution and results.[56] In the world of building a business, simply having the idea is just the first step. The reality of launching and growing a company is a matter of focus: you must be able to define where, when, and how to allocate energy and time in order to make progress.

Elisabeth Galperin, owner of Turn Leaf Organizing and mother of two boys, coaches her clients on how to master productivity in their businesses and lives. Her number one tip to a small business owner? The morning routine.

"It's about the process of setting up your time and your calendar so you can focus throughout the day. If you start out strong, you're more likely to stay on track."

---

54 Whitney Wolfe, "40 Entrepreneurs Share Their Secrets to Staying Focused," *Entrepreneur*, accessed May 22, 2019.

55 Jeffrey Hayzlett, "Why Focus Is the Number-One Element of Business Success," *Entrepreneur*, September 23, 2015.

56 Neil Patel, "How to Focus On What Matters as an Entrepreneur," *Inc.com*, February 19, 2015.

Staying focused on the minutes of the day is one piece of the focus puzzle. As Neil Patel, cofounder of Crazy Egg, explained:

"There are a million things to do in a startup. But most of those million tasks are a waste of time. The true essentials are few:

- Focus on building the business, not doing busywork.
- Focus on selling your product, not raising funding.
- Focus on doing things that empower you, not discourage you.
- Focus on listening to customers, not just critics.

This isn't an overwhelming list. That's the whole point—to focus. You'll never win at the mind game of business if you can't focus. It's time to start focusing on the most meaningful activities of all—things that grow and prosper your business."[57]

Many people have great ideas. In fact, *most* people have great ideas. As an avid networker for the first several years of my life (although less so now that I'm more *focused* on how I spend my time), I shook hands and chatted with hundreds of people, business owners and non-business owners alike. I was always genuinely entertained when a new acquaintance would share their "big idea" with me.

"Do you want to hear my business idea?" or "I've got a suggestion for another business for you."

---

57   Ibid.

If you network for your own business (or you have family members who love to brainstorm), you've heard it before. There are lots of ideas out there in the world! In fact, most of the high-performing people I know start additional businesses "for fun." When the COVID-19 pandemic of 2020 rendered many of my entrepreneurial friends across the world homebound, business ideas were firing like bullets.

I myself started entertaining a new project with two other entrepreneur friends. (In fact, I wrote most of this book during the COVID-19 outbreak!) But the reality is that having the idea and building the business are two separate things. The ability to focus on the task at hand and see it through is often significantly more challenging than we think, and it's an obstacle many business owners learn in their first several years at work.

When the pull of a million pieces of feedback and new ideas and children and to-do lists is persistent, staying focused on short-term tasks that lead to long-term goals is a superpower. Studies have proven women to be more productive in work environments than men.[58] Among women, professionals with children are more productive than those without children.[59]

"Mothers, in general, whether they're in the corporate setting or in their own business, they know how to focus and they don't get distracted," said Megan Flatt, a business coach

---

58 Robby Berman, "Women are more productive than men, according to new research," *World Economic Forum*, October 8, 2018.

59 Ylan Q Mui, "Study: Women with more children are more productive at work," *The Washington Post*, October 30, 2014.

for women entrepreneurs. "They know they don't have eight hours to devote to single tasks. They have forty minutes, and they know how to use that time. They're able to peel back the 'onion' of things to do and really get to the heart of what they need to be working on, and they can do that very quickly. They simply don't have the luxury of time because there are other people and responsibilities waiting for them outside of their work."

When the opportunity to do work or complete a task arises, Expectant Entrepreneurs set themselves up to quickly move into action. Shawna Navaro, owner of Innerspace creative design agency, knew that her productivity was best in three-hour blocks of time.

"I developed certain boundaries and guidelines to help, especially because I work from home. During the summers, my husband is also home while his school is on summer break, so we have our children home with us. I've learned that I need a three-hour minimum block of time to really be able to focus and complete a task."

Shawna's life certainly doesn't happen in three-hour increments, but having learned how and where she focuses best, she is able to set herself up for success when she does schedule a three-hour opportunity to get creative and accomplish what needs to be accomplished. Then she switches focus when her available time is up.

"No one has less time than a mom," said Kate Torgersen of Milk Stork. "When I started Milk Stork, I had no free time. I built that business when I was hooked up to a pump because

it was the only 'free' time I had. I built the business in twenty-minute increments three to five times a day. I actually found that as a working mother, my relationship to work improved after children because I knew the value of each block of time."[60]

The ability to focus is significant. It means effective control over time as well as effective control over energy—both highly valued commodities in the life of an Expectant Entrepreneur.

---

60 Kate Torgerson, "What Motherhood Taught this CEO About Starting a Business," Interview by IDEO, May 6, 2020.

14

Self-Awareness

THE REALIZATION THAT WE ARE JUST MERE

HUMANS FULL OF FLAWS AND WONDER.

"I think we're the coolest. We're self-aware of what we are and what we want to do."

Jill Salzman ought to know about business-owning moms. She's built a business called the Founding Moms that develops local communities of mom-entrepreneurs. In addition to being a Founding Mom herself, Jill interacts with and observes other founding moms daily.

"I know that there's a similarity among the people who join the Founding Moms, so it's not reflecting of all business-owning mothers. I know that I choose to see particular things in these women, but I think we're amazing. I like that we are self-aware."

Expectant Entrepreneurs seem to share a certain amount of candid realization of their own humanity. Some of it was learned by experience: they've failed, struggled, rebuilt,

changed plans, and succeeded in their own ways dozens of times in both business and motherhood. Some of it was a bit more *je ne sais quoi*: an implicit understanding that being ourselves means being vulnerable, open to feedback, and forthcoming with emotions.

One standout aspect of self-awareness in Expectant Entrepreneurs is a sense of pride in being women with ambitions. We know we hold ourselves to high standards, and we take ownership of meeting those standards. There's an underlying presence of goal-getting and personal responsibility in building the life that we envision for ourselves and our families. Rather than wait for others to take the lead and create an opportunity for us, we're unapologetic about moving forward.

As previously explored, Kate Torgerson, founder of Milk Stork, felt a strong desire to get back to work after her twins were born.

"I really wanted to be back invested in this other part of my personality and that was my professional ambitions," Kate said. On that work trip, Kate discovered the need to have a travel solution for breastfeeding moms, and she had the idea for the business that would become Milk Stork on the return flight home.[61]

---

61   Kate Torgerson, "What Motherhood Taught This CEO About Starting a Business," IDEO U Webinar, May 6, 2020.

Rachel Murphy, a certified life coach, has observed a practical challenge to self-awareness that Expectant Entrepreneurs seem to have in common.

"I think that when women approach problems with an entrepreneurial mindset, we are good at recognizing what we're good at and what we're not good at. We have a quick self-awareness in that sense. But what's different is that in our position as entrepreneurs rather than as an executive, for instance, is that we seem to want to try to learn how to do *all the things*. We decide it's up to us to fix those things that we're not good at by taking a course, trying harder, struggling through. I believe we have a harder time letting go at first. We know that we're controlling everything—even those things we're not great at—but it might take us a bit longer to let go and accept help."

Samantha Leenheer, owner of Samantha Joy Events, reflected on her time as a new mom and a business owner. Samantha had her first child during the COVID-19 pandemic, which significantly impacted her business and her ability to have the maternity leave she had planned for.

"Looking back, I think I would have probably asked for more help. I think as a business owner, we just don't always ask for help. I think you don't mind asking for help from other people who you think are like like-minded and trustworthy, but I would have just asked for help from anyone and everyone. There's a reason the phrase 'it takes a village' exists."

Self-awareness requires the ability to look inward and understand your own limits. Despite what many Expectant

Entrepreneurs want to believe, we are not machines. Until I had my first daughter, my work limits were nearly nonexistent. I had no boundaries and worked all days of the week, and sometimes all hours of the day. My self-care was exercise, and that was it. Being able to truly relax was a mystery to me. When my daughter was born, she forced me to slow down, and I resented it at first.

With time, I realized that one of my reactions during times of stress is to dive deeper into work. Working is where I feel the most confident, most able, and in control. Having a baby challenges our ability to identify our needs. How much can we truly take on before our bodies and minds begin to suffer? After AJ arrived, I went through a bit of an ambling journey through self-awareness, and I'm still on it now. There are aspects of who I am that are clear and consistent. There are other things, like how to be still, to fully listen and be present, and how to care for my mental health, that I constantly explore. I'm not the only one.

"On this journey of being an entrepreneur-mom, I've been able to identify who those important people are in my life that are willing to give me feedback and support me when I need it," said Nikki Laub, owner of Premiere Concrete Supply. "My sons are part of that group of people, and I jokingly call them my board of directors because they keep me straight."

The idea of self-awareness is not that we're fully aware of all of the aspects of who we are as humans. It's that we *know that we don't know*. Being able to change, to gather new information and make different decisions as a result, to relate to people who are different than ourselves, admit to weaknesses,

celebrate strengths—these are all essential components of self-awareness.

15

Resilience

———

All of Marie Englesson's investors failed her.

Marie's story, like all of the women's stories in this book, fits into several themes, and resilience is certainly one of them. In 2011, Marie launched Atsoko, a distributor of high-quality makeup and beauty products, in Tanzania. She broke barriers to providing women in Tanzania access to European brands that otherwise were not available in local stores. Marie's inspiration to build Atsoko came from her women colleagues at her previous workplace, a telecommunications company that operated in Tanzania and Rwanda.

"I had a number of female colleagues at Tigo and whenever I went to Europe they'd ask me to bring them products they

couldn't get hold of," she said in a 2015 article documenting her business's growth.[62]

In 2018, Marie learned she was pregnant with her first child. At the time, her business was in need of funding, particularly if Marie was going to take a maternity leave of any kind. She was the acting CEO, and she would need to hire a replacement.

"All of the investors I approached told me to reach back out to them when I was back from maternity leave," Marie said. "In the end, all of the external investors said the same thing. They wanted to invest in the entrepreneur as a person, which was me, and not necessarily the business itself. Plus, a pregnancy indicated a red flag to them about my commitment level to the business."

Marie either needed to scale up the business or exit it all together, and her experience with investors created an exit plan for her next move. In the end, she sold Atsoko and temporarily moved back to Sweden, her home country, to have her son and take advantage of the generous maternity leave laws. Marie successfully sold the business, which is still in operations today, and now works as a consultant for companies across the world.

The transition away from Atsoko was not, in fact, a failure for Marie. She knew the financials of the business, and she knew that there was a decision that needed to happen. Becoming

---

62 Marie Englesson, interview by Dinfin Mulupi, "Meet the Swedish entrepreneur who saw the potential for cosmetics in Tanzania," *Africa Business Insight,* March 31, 2015.

a mother altered her future in Atsoko, but it also opened up a new path forward.

Grit. Hustle. Persistence. These are all aspects of the same quality of continuing to move forward, despite resistance or challenges. Resilience is our ability to see the big picture, look beyond a temporary setback, and keep going, even when the situation isn't ideal or perfectly clear.

"One of my favorite stories of being a mom-entrepreneur was when I pitched my business to my local bank. I had my ten-month-old daughter, and at this point, she came everywhere with me in my business," said Maria Friström, owner of a real estate development company in Finland. "I was looking for any kind of loan, just hoping for an investment of some kind. So I did what we know what to do as women who own businesses: I prepared like a maniac."

Maria arrived at the bank with her laptop, her daughter, and her purse, and she delivered her pitch magnificently. She was in the zone, so much so that she was fully focused on her pitch and temporarily lost track of her daughter, who was playing on the floor.

"As soon as I was done with the pitch, I was like, 'Where's the baby?!'" Maria recalled. "During that time, she had wreaked havoc in the room. She was under the table, there was food everywhere. She had played with a sanitary pad that was in my purse, torn business stickers apart, and generally caused a huge mess."

Maria left with a five hundred thousand-euro loan.

Resilience is powerful. It motivates women like Maria to pack up everything she needed (*Why do babies need so much stuff?*), get to the bank with her baby in tow, and land a significant loan for her business. Resilience is the ability to look at the surface of the situation, see the distractions and challenges, and decide "I can do it anyway." The skill to keep moving takes time and practice, and it gets easier when we define our values and keep the big picture in mind.

When Genna Gardner, owner of Elevate Digital, was preparing for the arrival of her third son, she knew that disclosing the fact that she was expecting might impact the acquisition of new clients.

"At this point in my life and career, if someone doesn't want to work with me because I have children, that's okay with me," Genna said. "I can go and find new clients that will be perfectly happy to have a mom of three boys working on their business."

On paper, this might seem like a simple decision. *Of course we don't want to work with people who mind that we have children.* But in reality, letting go of potential clients or current paying clients is difficult to do, especially at the beginning stages of business when money is tight. Resilience allows us to do what feels right for ourselves and our businesses. It keeps us continually seeking new and different ways to build a life and a business we envision for ourselves—and to keep moving toward that vision no matter what challenges come up.

"It takes a certain kind of work ethic, a certain bit of grit, and a certain kind of person to be a mother who runs a business," said Nikki Laub, owner of Premiere Concrete Supply. "Sometimes we have to push a little harder for things to happen and achieve the goals that we set out to achieve, and some days are harder than others. I give myself permission to not feel guilty about the decision to sometimes prioritize motherhood or work, because I remember that my sons are watching. I keep moving forward every day, and as long as I can lay down at night and feel good about being a mom and feel good about my business, I'm good with that."

Resilience is motherhood: going through the hard decisions, the challenging days, and the transitions for the sake of growth and your family's well-being. Resilience is being an entrepreneur who is willing to try, fail, and keep going for the vision you see for yourself and your company.

We are resilient.

16

Risk Tolerance

LEARNING TO BE UNCOMFORTABLE WITH
THE POTENTIAL OF FAILURE.

In one corner of the ring, we have the blood-pressure rising, sleepless-night causing, unpredictable RISK!

In the other corner, facing off, we have the daydream-inducing, pride-fueling, tantalizing REWARD!

The duel between risk and reward seemed to battle it out for the entirety of each of my pregnancies. How I felt about my business changed as quickly as a boxer throws punches. I was working so hard to make the reward possible: a maternity leave that was financially secure, flexible, and supported by a business that was carrying on and making money without me. In reaching for that reward, I was jumping headfirst into the risk associated with it: significant financial impact, the lack of a maternity leave due to the need to stay active in the business, and a team that felt unsupported and confused.

Both options, in my mind, were equally possible. The truth was that the reward was much stronger than the risk in this match. I had spent years building my business and slowly making the risks weaker and weaker as I put more and more effort into achieving my goals for my business. Like many, if not all, of the entrepreneurs I know, I conveniently forgot about those years of effort and training. Everything still felt risky to me, despite the fact that I had grown a stable business that was significantly more likely to be completely unfazed by my absence for six weeks than it was to implode in the same amount of time.

Part of the existence of being an entrepreneur is taking a risk: starting something new, investing your time and your money, putting your ideas out to the market, and being vulnerable to rejection. Being okay with the potential of failure is the risk that nearly every entrepreneur makes at some point. Some choose a risky start by leaving comfortable jobs to begin their own business. Others make the choice later to risk scaling instead of staying as a one-person business. Some entrepreneurs risk more by adding to their product line.

Whether we're standing up for our core values or changing the way we do business, entrepreneurship is rife with risk. For those of us who choose to pursue a business despite the risk, the possibility of reward is greater. For some of us, it might be just slightly greater, and for others, the reward feels obvious and huge. Regardless, we've all deemed the potential reward to be life-changing, and so we change our lives.

"It's okay to be a little bit scared," Kate Torgerson said.

"Within ten days of launching the business, I was contacted by one of the largest consulting firms in the country who asked us to bring Milk Stork on as a benefit to their North American employees. I will never forget this call. I was in my minivan in the childcare parking lot, and I took the call. She said, 'We have forty thousand employees in North America, and we want to offer Milk Stork as a benefit. Can you launch a program for us in thirty days?' And I just remember saying, 'Yes. Thank you,' and deciding that I would just figure it out."[63]

Choosing to be an entrepreneur is choosing to be okay with risk and developing a tolerance for it along the way. Choosing to be a mother is also choosing to be okay with risk.

Motherhood, as natural as it may seem, carries risks of many varieties. Simply the decision of wanting to create a family faces the potential of failure. Nearly 12 percent of all couples who are trying to have children cannot due to infertility.[64] Research shows that between 10 and 20 percent of all medically confirmed pregnancies end in miscarriage.[65] There are risks to the mother that increase with every pregnancy, and those risks become more prevalent if you add in factors like age, weight, and lifestyle.

Beyond the physical risk, every mother experiences her own definition of risk and reward in motherhood. What does it

---

63   Kate Torgerson, "What Motherhood Taught This CEO About Starting a Business," IDEO U Webinar, May 6, 2020.

64   Kristin L. Rooney and Alice D. Domar, "The relationship between stress and infertility," *Dialogues in Clinical Neuroscience* 20, no. 1 (March 2018): 41-47.

65   Mayo Clinic, "Miscarriage: Symptoms and Causes," accessed May 26, 2020.

mean to succeed as a mother? What does it mean to fail as a mother?

"What I'm seeing across the world is that mother-entrepreneurs have two things in common: they're living with massive amounts of fear about failure and letting their family down and the guilt that we feel as mothers," said Jill Salzman, founder of the Founding Moms, which offers meetups for entrepreneurial mothers across the world. "I see this both universally and internationally and in a variety of cultures."

There is so much to explore with the thoughts and concepts of failure. In a question, is failure ever a fact? Expectant entrepreneurs may *feel* afraid or nervous about becoming mothers or taking the leap into entrepreneurship. But afraid is a *feeling*, and feelings aren't facts. When we empower ourselves to be in our own business, we define our own versions of success and failure, which means we can change them, too.

Part 3

How to Be
an Expectant
Entrepreneur

17

How to Be an Expectant Entrepreneur

———

The following stories and pages are my vision for my own contribution to the Expectant Entrepreneur community. I was searching for something like this: a checklist or a mental guide to help me think through all of the larger decisions that I needed to make in the coming months before the arrival of my second daughter.

As I moved through my pregnancy, I wanted a fellow business-owning mother who had been in this position to be my sounding board. Was I thinking about all of the important things? Was I making decisions with enough time?

From the first trimester until my daughter Lena was born, I felt like I had made more decisions than I had in the several years leading up to my second pregnancy. All of a sudden, I was in action mode and wanted to plan and prepare like I never quite had before. I documented the swirling chamber of thoughts that I had throughout that time with notes to

myself, voice recordings I made while I drove to and from meetings, and a notebook full of ideas and decisions.

The goal now is to offer my thoughts as a way for other women to check their own. In no way is my experience comprehensive of every other woman's journey. That is impossible. Our paths to motherhood and through business ownership will be unique and interesting. But what *is* possible is simply to share my experience and offer reflections on my lessons learned in the event they help even just one other business owner navigate this specific, beautiful, complicated, and stressful time in life.

18

The First Trimester

———

My digital pregnancy test left very little room for interpretation. That day was a Monday, and I was pregnant for the second time. Adam and I had another child on the radar, yet seeing the positive test still took my breath away. I was simultaneously overjoyed and overwhelmed right from the start.

That morning, I had raced from my bed to the gym to CVS and back home before heading to work. I slowed my body and brain enough during that morning hustle to take the pregnancy test I had just purchased. The test was intended to simply make sure that I wasn't *actually* pregnant as I was heading into a grand slam of a business month. The Monday I found out I was pregnant was the beginning of a month packed with back-to-back business trips to both Seattle and Toronto, a personal trip to the beach for a long weekend away with Adam, and a speaking engagement in front of several hundred people for a local women-owned business conference.

In the instant after getting the positive pregnancy test, my brain shifted my upcoming schedule from admittedly busy

to completely overwhelming. Welcome to the first trimester as an Expectant Entrepreneur.

Depending on how far along you are in your pregnancy, by the time you realize you're pregnant, the first trimester may actually be the shortest trimester once you finally start counting weeks. But despite its comparative brevity, the first trimester has an enormous impact. From wrapping our minds around the fact that a baby is coming to sharing news with partners and spouses to beginning to plan for the months ahead, a pregnancy infiltrates our thoughts, decisions, and businesses.

In the context of pregnancy and business, I found that my first-trimester thoughts most generally fell into a handful of areas. This is by no means a comprehensive list of everything that we, as business owners, might need to think about. But from the perspective of an Expectant Entrepreneur, this list comprises my most persistent thoughts.

First-Trimester Focus:

- Finances
- Health Care and Insurance
- Physical Changes
- Communicating with Clients: How Much to Share
- Planning Ahead
- Finding Your EE Community

FINANCES

In honor of the amazing women I met who opened up to me for the sake of this book and project, I am going to be fully transparent: money is by far my largest source of anxiety. In fact, as I write this book, I'm in a money coaching program to revisit how I think about money and manage it in both my business and my household. It's definitely *a thing* for me.

Money has a tendency to dominate my thoughts: *Am I making enough money? I should be making more. I should definitely be saving more. I should have less debt. How can I make more?* And during my time as an Expectant Entrepreneur, my money mind went into overdrive: *How am I ever going to be able to afford a maternity leave? How will I be able to make money while I'm out? I can't take time off. I need more people—can I afford more people? How much do I need to save for the birth? How much will day care cost?*

Money mindset is powerful. As Jen Sincero writes in her book *You Are a Badass at Making Money: Master the Mindset of Wealth,* "Money is one of the most loaded topics out there— we love money, hate money, obsess over money, ignore money, resent money, hoard money, crave money, bad-mouth money, money is rife with so much desire and shame and weirdness it's a wonder we can utter the word above a whisper, let alone go out and joyfully rake it in."[66]

Of all the characteristics of Expectant Entrepreneurs this book explores, the one characteristic I have found most

---

66 Jen Sincero, *You are a Badass at Making Money: Master the Mindset of Wealth* (Philadelphia: Penguin, 2017), 1.

powerful in these women is the ability to move forward and make big decisions without knowing exactly how. I'm here to tell you this: you *will* figure out the money. Even if it seems scarce and your cash flow leaves no room for even a single unaccounted for penny, you are going to make a plan and figure out how to make it work. You have a 100 percent success rate so far. You will do it again.

The first trimester is a perfect time to prepare your finances for the year ahead. I found the following items important for the early stages of exploring my financials:

- Household monthly income and expenses
- Business monthly income and expenses
- Health care costs and a best guess as to how they'll change with a new baby
- Upcoming large payments (like taxes)
- Any foreseeable changes to your budget due to a new baby (a new car, for instance)

I also made a mental note about the systems that were working for my family and any I wanted to change. For instance, my family was making a shift to stop using all credit cards and pay only with the money we had in our accounts in an effort to reduce credit card debt. This was working for us, and I wanted to keep it going as best we could. As a result, I wanted to try to estimate how much to save to pay for health care expenses connected to the birth. This is also a great time to remind you that most health care systems offer interest-free payment plans for large health-related expenses, and I used this option to reduce the need to save a large amount of cash for those bills in particular.

Some important questions to consider:

- What is working well in my home or business related to money?
- How much do I *want* to save to cover medical bills? How much do I *need* to save to cover medical bills?
- Where do I have room to reduce expenses?
- Do I need to adjust my income? Is this realistic to plan now, should I reevaluate in a few months?

As the financial provider for my household, I often want to try to plan out my finances as far in advance as possible. The reality is, as a business owner who works on projects and short-term contracts, this is very challenging to do.

I recently listened to a train-of-thought recording I created at the beginning of my pregnancy as I was fretting about my finances. I was rounding up expenses, making calls to my insurance provider, reaching out to hospitals, and doing my best to get a realistic number of what I was going to be on the hook to pay. For the record, I ended up overpredicting my expenses by a whopping eleven thousand dollars, and most of those errors can be attributed to worry. I hear the anxiety in my own voice as I listened back, and I just wanted to go back and tell myself everything is going to be okay.

In the first trimester of my second pregnancy, I knew there was no way for me to accurately predict where my business was going to be in eight or nine months. I had to work hard to let go of my natural craving to know *exactly* what things would look like when the baby arrived—trying to plan was an exercise in futility. If you have the ability to predict your

finances due to the types of contracts you have with clients, great! If you do not, you don't have to know right now. In the first trimester, focus on what you do know and what you can control right now: understanding your numbers, facing your finances, assessing any changes that need to be made, and making a plan to change them.

HEALTH CARE AND INSURANCE

My husband is an amazing father and caregiver to our girls. This is a fact in my life. It's also a fact that I have daydreamed about him returning to work simply for the employee benefits, specifically health insurance. Between my first pregnancy and my second, our coverage options changed dramatically. We purchased our health care from the Health Insurance Marketplace, but there are lots of innovative solutions to getting the coverage that you want and need.

The first trimester is a great time to examine your insurance plan to better understand your coverage, regardless of whether you buy directly from the provider or you are covered by a spouse's plan. Knowing whether your preferred doctors or care providers are considered in network is a great first step. If your preferred physician is not on your plan, you may need to shop around for an OB-GYN or another provider who is in network. Plus, most plans outline what they do and do not cover for maternal health to help you better understand how costs are calculated and what would be an additional or elective expense for you, such as additional ultrasounds.

With the number of doctor visits and checkups in the months ahead, your coverage will be important to determine early on. Unfortunately, the United States underperforms in maternal health compared to other developed nations, particularly for women of color.

According to the Maternal Health Task Force at the Harvard T. H. Chan School of Public Health Center of Excellence in Maternal and Child Health, Black women die at a rate that ranges from three to four times the rate of their white counterparts, and approximately 25 percent of all US women do not receive the recommended number of prenatal visits.[67] This number rises to 32 percent among African Americans and to 41 percent among Native American or Alaska Native women.[68]

While you may not be able to switch plans before your baby is born, having a baby *does* qualify you for a Special Enrollment Period (SEP), which means you can enroll in coverage or change your coverage for a certain amount of time.

If you are not enrolled in or not interested in traditional insurance from the government's Health Insurance Marketplace or a private insurance provider, there are other options. Consider health care sharing ministries to help cover costs,

67 "Trends in Pregnancy-Related Death: Pregnancy Mortality Surveillance System," U.S. Centers for Disease Control and Prevention, last modified September 25, 2020.
68 "Healthy people 2010: Understanding and improving health," Department of Health, Human Services, Washington, DC., Healthy People 2010 (Group), and United States Government Printing Office, 2000.

but be sure to research what is covered and what is not by alternative forms of health care coverage.

Your health matters, and your child's health matters.

PHYSICAL CHANGES

"I am tired all the time."

If you are a goddess among mortals and had minimal physical complaints in your first trimester, feel free to take your well-rested, well-fed, clear-headed self to the next section. To the rest of us, *I feel you.*

Katie Garry was hit hard by the absolute exhaustion that experienced in her first trimester with her third child. Katie, on any given day, is not a two-hour nap kind of CEO. She's an Expectant Entrepreneur with two other children and a growing business: naps are a luxury. But during her first trimester, which coincided with the mentally and emotionally exhausting spring and early summer of 2020, when there was a global pandemic and racial reckonings across the United States, there was nothing she could do but allow her body to rest.

"I will take a two-hour nap in the middle of the day, and I still wake up tired."

Exhaustion is real. It's a reality for many entrepreneurs and mothers. Layering in the recommendation to reduce caffeine intake while pregnant leaves even the most aggressive among us face down in a pillow in the middle of a sunny afternoon.

When Shawna Navaro, owner of a creative design company called Innerspace, learned she was pregnant with her third child, she knew what to anticipate: feeling sick at all hours of the day and being so exhausted that she felt like she had to peel herself away from the bed in an effort to at least check her email for any urgent issues.

"My morning sickness is pretty all-consuming," she said. "It's hard to do anything for myself, my family, or my business. When I think back on it, I honestly don't know how I did it."

For me, the worst was the horrible, blur-my-vision headaches that simply would not go away for days, no matter what I drank or ate or how much I slept. Sleep escapes me during pregnancy, leaving me up in the middle of the night, thinking about how desperately I want to go back to sleep—a vicious cycle.

Pregnancy is many, many things—one of which is a *very* physical process that each of us experiences differently. As this book explores, Expectant Entrepreneurs are typically persistent, resilient, creative, and focused. Becoming pregnant can, in a single swoop, render us exhausted, fuzzy-brained, and distracted (at best). Keeping a business afloat when your body is demanding so much from you can feel impossible.

As an Expectant Entrepreneur, if you are facing the physical demands of pregnancy, here are some things to consider:

- First and foremost, give yourself some space to accept that your body is in control. To the best of your ability, give it what it needs. Stay hydrated, rest, repeat.

- Adjust your work schedule to better align with times you can work effectively. Reminder: your ability to control your time and your calendar is one of the perks of owning your own business! If there was ever a time to be generous and flexible with your schedule for your own well-being, this is it.
- Create a work environment that offers you space to rest when you need to. My office has a small utility closet that we turned into a phone booth and meditation corner, and I routinely went in there to just shut my eyes for ten minutes at a time. Find ways to make this easier for yourself.
- Beyond that, if you have a team of people, now is a great time to lean on others to see how they can manage while you are out of office.
- If you don't have a team of people, now is also a great time to think about who you might love to have on your team. If you could offload tasks right now, what would they be? Look into hiring someone who can do those tasks for you, or write that role down for later action.

One of the hardest and also the best parts of being pregnant is that your body takes over. Although one of your habits might be working ten or more hours in a day, the reality is that your body will likely force you to change that habit. This is frustrating in the moment, but on the flip side, learning how to get more done in less time is going to be even more important once the baby arrives. This is a good time to explore when you're at your best, adjust client expectations about turnaround time, and consider how to outsource to other people to make your business run more smoothly and effectively.

COMMUNICATING WITH CLIENTS: HOW MUCH TO SHARE

I'm not necessarily proud to admit this, but I spent an embarrassing amount of time in my first trimester figuring out how to handle communicating my news with clients. I had constant internal battle of thoughts about when to reveal I was pregnant, and this would be a recurring theme throughout the duration of my pregnancy. At the core of the issue was determining *who* needs to know *what* and *when* they need to know it.

One of my clients is in the music industry, which is so fun. From live music events to touring independent music venues, there's never a shortage of interesting and new social opportunities with the work. My clients are passionate, music-loving people, and I genuinely enjoy being with them. As excited as I was to be expecting another child, I was also disappointed that my vision for my first trip to Toronto for Canadian Music Week was going to be different than I had anticipated.

I had set my own expectations to continue the socializing aspect of this particular work trip. I knew we were going to do a lot of brainstorming in dimly lit bars with sticky floors and the lovely smell of stale beer—a surprisingly great ambiance to get creative.

Rather than participate in the delightfully buzzed conversations, I knew I was going to have to fight against my tiredness and hang out after a full workday for as long as I could—both out of desire to take advantage of the time with my clients as well as to accomplish some of our goals for our time together.

But all of this took place before I felt comfortable sharing I was pregnant.

At the time, I was only about eight or nine weeks along, which just felt too soon to share. I wanted to hit that important twelve-week milestone before I went down the path of bringing clients into my journey with me. I had a bit of a self-created dilemma ahead: Do I offer white lies about my sleepiness and lack of drinking? Do I fake it with mocktails and nonalcoholic beverages? Do I mention that I'm not feeling well? Do I blame it on a new medication or recovery from a stomach bug?

Both sides of the coin exhausted me. On one hand, my husband and I didn't want to share the news too soon for a variety of reasons. Simply the thought of having a miscarriage and then having to share that story with my clients was emotionally draining. On the other hand, I was either pretending or white-lying for several days in a row. As a person who doesn't particularly hide things well, this was also exhausting and felt like a lot of work.

In the end, I ended up not bringing much attention to my situation and just casually drank club sodas and nonalcoholic cocktails. I was incredibly well hydrated my whole trip due to the amount of club soda with lime I consumed each night. If my clients noticed, they didn't say anything. What's more likely is that they rightfully didn't notice (my beverage selection is not particularly newsworthy even when it involved alcohol), and all the hours I spent determining how to handle the situation were unnecessary. But in the moment, deciding which way to go was hard.

Looking back, I realize I could have made my life a lot easier by not overthinking the situation: my rule was going to be to stay quiet about my family's news with clients until my twelve-week mark, and then we would feel more comfortable talking about the pregnancy. Until then, just be the lovely, nondrinking version of myself.

If you are figuring out how to communicate with clients, there are a few things to consider as you set your own guidelines:

- Most importantly, this is your choice. You can tell the whole world the moment you find out you're pregnant if you want to. You can also wait to share the news with anyone at all, and even then, just take it on a person-by-person or client-by-client basis. There are no rules, and you cannot break them.
- By and large, of all the women I spoke with, the majority of them had great experiences sharing their news with clients. Many women reported feeling additional levels of support from clients, particularly women clients, after disclosing their news.
- You do not have to tell all people at the same time.

What's important is that you feel comfortable with your decision. I found making the decision one time easiest: I am not sharing this news with any clients until I'm at least twelve weeks along, and after that will be a case-by-case situation. After I made the decision once, it was done and I was able to move along on my merry, business-owning way. You might want to feel out the situation and make a call in the moment. Whatever you decide to do, you don't *owe* anyone any information. This is your body, your business, and your decision.

PLANNING AHEAD

If there's one recommendation I can make for any Expectant Entrepreneur in the first trimester, it's to start planning your planning time. Make room in your calendar each week or every other week to have a CEO day in which you do less (or no) client work and instead work on your own business. In the coming months, there's a lot of work to be done, increasingly frequent doctor's appointments, and plenty of other demands on your already pressed time. If you don't have time blocked out to do your planning, the time will slip away.

CEO days are all about thinking big-picture, making decisions, implementing systems, and building your team, not about how to solve a specific client or project challenge. Giving yourself room to think and get creative in your own business is hard enough—when you couple it with being on a forty-week (or less) time frame, having CEO days is incredibly impactful.

There are a lot of resources available for how to structure a great CEO day. From the perspective of an Expectant Entrepreneur, some of the themes and topics covered in this book would be great topics to cover in your own CEO day. Consider scheduling days in your calendar that are devoted to exploring your:

- Team: Who is your team? Who do you need to get rid of? Who do you need to keep?
- Information: What is in your head that you need to transfer to a document or system? Being the only person who understands your business is not helpful to your or to

anyone who might want to step in to help you. Do you have or need training manuals for your business?

- Finances: Get to know your numbers. Understand your cash flow and explore the financial questions posed earlier in this chapter.
- Physical Environment: Do you need to create changes in your working environment? Move offices? Create a different space in your home for your business? File paperwork away that's been sitting in a pile on your desk or in that file folder in your bag for months?
- Contacts: Do you have updated information on all of your clients and your team members documented in a place that's accessible for other people?
- Time/Calendar: Can you plan when you'll be taking off for maternity leave and make a guess as to when you'll be back?
- Goals: What are your goals for the next six to nine months? Do you have goals and deadlines you want or need to meet before your baby is born?

Make time to build your business and prepare it for the arrival of your child. Even if this is your fifth child or beyond, a baby will impact you and your business. Give yourself time to plan and get creative. And bonus: if you build this habit during pregnancy, it's also a great one to keep once you're back at work!

FINDING YOUR EE COMMUNITY

One of the challenges I encountered on my journey as an Expectant Entrepreneur was finding women like me. When I was pregnant with AJ, I simply didn't know as many small

business owners. I had a handful of personal friends in my life who were already mothers, and they were vital to me. Let's be honest: becoming a mom in any stage or phase of life is made significantly better with the support and "been-there-done-that" knowledge of other mothers. While my personal friends and family were incredibly supportive, I found myself longing for someone who truly and deeply understood what I was going through as a new mom and business owner.

To get vulnerable for a moment, during my first pregnancy, my range of emotions about becoming a mom and also running a business were scary and new. Even on my best days, here's a very high-level recap of everything I was feeling—and yes, they're embarrassing to write out and uncomfortable to share:

Envy: I was hands-down envious of women who had corporate-paid maternity leave. No matter if it was six weeks or twelve, I deeply wanted the security of knowing I had a job, income, benefits, and whatever else comes with a typical maternity leave (like, an office baby shower? I'm assuming those are a thing. I really let my imagination fly with how green the other side of the maternity leave field was).

Resentment: I am not going to be pretend to be a higher person here. I, at first, felt *very* sorry for myself. Why didn't I get the experience of sitting at home on a fluffy bed, nursing my newborn in a cloud of white pillows, wearing a satin robe and being blissfully happy? Why did I have to think about business while I was supposed to be thinking only about my baby?

These are the beautiful visions of a woman who had not yet experienced childbirth and recovery from it. As I quickly learned, maternity leave is significantly less glamorous and way less restful than I ever imagined. But I didn't know the difference, and I sometimes resented my own choice to become a business owner. Somehow, I felt I had been denied this restful maternity leave I was owed.

Financial Insecurity: How was I supposed to provide for my family if I was also supposed to be growing and feeding a new human? I craved an enormous pot of gold that would simply pop up and exist for me and provide me with enough money to not worry about money. What a dream! I wanted heaps of cash in the bank and flush retirement and savings accounts. I wanted signed contracts and locked deals and the security of knowing that money was coming in, regardless of the hours I did (or did not) clock that week.

Fear: I certainly experienced days when I was afraid of becoming a mother. I was afraid of giving up the independence that had been absolutely vital to the launch and growth of my business. I was afraid of giving up time I spent working on my business or on myself, like time in the gym and with friends. I was nervous about what the birth would be like, and I decided very early on I would have an epidural with AJ (I chose differently with Lena). I was afraid of failure on all fronts: failure in business, failure as a mom, failure as a leader. Fear ran deep.

That was real. Those emotions were present at any given moment. But, thankfully, they were balanced by a conduit of positive feelings and emotions, too.

Freedom: I was absolutely thrilled by the freedom that my life provided me. I was free to work from my couch in the middle of the night when pregnancy insomnia grabbed hold. I was free to decide who I wanted to work with, how much to charge, and when to begin or end working relationships. I was free to take AS MUCH TIME as I wanted! If I truly wanted to, I could plan to take months off of work. I was free to travel and spend time with my family at any given moment. I was free to take days off when I felt sick and work very long hours when I was in the flow.

Gratitude: I had a husband who was willing to be a stay-at-home dad. I had created a lifestyle that enabled me to live with flexibility. My partner and I were able to conceive children. I had very easy pregnancies, all things considered. I had a body that knew what to do with a growing child. I had a home that had enough space for us to live safely and comfortably and that was complete with a home office. I had a dog who was my constant companion and an exceptionally good listener. I had a family who lived nearby, and friends who love me. I had a growing community of fellow business owners who gave good advice and saw my potential, even when I could not.

Unlimited Earning Potential: I could make as much money as I wanted. I had built a business that was strong enough to allow my husband to quit his job and stay home to care for our daughters. I had enough money to pay for insurance and health care costs. I had the potential to bring on as many clients as I wanted at whatever price I wanted. There was no limit to the amount of money I could have.

Excitement: I was going to be a mom! We were going to be parents! I was so excited to bring a new little person into our lives and our marriage. I couldn't wait to meet her, and I was thrilled to be continuing the next generation of our families. I was excited to add a new dimension to my life that complemented who I already was as an individual. There was so much to be excited about.

These emotions, and so many more, were a very real part of my experience in both pregnancies, but particularly during my first. Like all moms do, I figured out how to manage them. In my case, the positive emotions outweighed the negative ones as a whole, and I'm aware that for some mothers, the emotions can be hard enough to manage without layering the actual work, planning, physical changes, and other aspects of pregnancy and entrepreneurship on top of it all.

In every Expectant Entrepreneur's journey, there will be a need for community: women who had walked this business-owning walk and grown their families and came out on the other side with their own lessons learned.

In the three and a half years between my girls, I worked hard to fill my life with women who could speak to their experience and support me on my own journey. By the time Lena was born, I had actually helped formed a local organization that gathers women entrepreneurs who are, or who want to be, mothers. I was part of a mastermind group of women business owners, the majority of whom were also mothers.

When you start to look around, you'll see that women are finding and forming their own small Expectant Entrepreneur

communities. It might be as small as two friends or as large as a big national network of business-owning moms. If you look, you will begin to see that Expectant Entrepreneurs everywhere are seeking one another out for support.

From mastermind groups to online communities to local networking organizations, there are women out there who know what you're feeling, understand your situation, and are ready to help and support. Reach out, ask for help, and connect!

19

The Second Trimester

I could not stop sweating, and not because of the pregnancy, despite being in my second trimester in the stifling heat of an Ohio summer. On any other day, my pregnancy *was* the reason I would be sweating (there's no heat like the heat of a pregnant woman in business clothes on a humid summer day). I was sweating because I was about to ask for a contract renewal from my largest client, and I was nervous.

For my entire ninety-minute drive up I-71 in the cornfields of Ohio, I was having an internal debate: *Do I share that my six-month renewal was going to include time that I personally was going to be out on maternity leave? Do I leave that part out, secure the deal, and then casually mention I'm pregnant? Was doing that somehow deceiving them of important information in their decision?*

My business friends encouraged me to act like a man: would a man be tentative about sharing an announcement that his wife was going to have a baby? More than likely, he would not be nervous about that piece of information impacting

a potential contract renewal. It would be an afterthought, although a baby would likely impact him in a significant way.

But the reality is that it's not the same. During the second trimester, my body was bound to betray any untold secrets as my belly popped out. I also would have to start realistically planning my team and my systems for the coming months. If everything went according to plan, there would be introductions and then handoffs of certain tasks to other people. I recognize that while I didn't *owe* anyone an explanation, there was also great joy in preparing for a baby. I wanted to share!

In the end, I weighed my options, and I decided not to share my news about my pregnancy during the same conversation about the contract renewal. They committed to another six months, and the next week during a conference call with the same people, I shared my news. Everyone was incredibly excited and had kind words to share. There were no questions about how work was going to be done, who was going to be doing it, or what my plans were for my business. None. They simply trusted me as a professional to make it work, which is exactly what my second trimester was focused on.

To me, the second trimester proved to be both the most important and the most productive. There wasn't the sense of rushing that creeps in during the third trimester, but there was a general sense of needing to work through my checklist. That checklist was ever-changing, but during the second trimester, business thoughts were focused on a handful of topics.

Second Trimester Focus:

- Team Planning and Outsourcing
- Creating Systems
- Pipeline of Work
- Communicating with Clients
- Planning Ahead

TEAM PLANNING AND OUTSOURCING

One of the most surprising things to me about owning a business was a near-immediate need to have a basic understanding of every aspect of running a business. By the time I officially started Verano in the spring of 2013, I was already fulfilling all of the roles that are critical for a strong company: sales, marketing, accounting, financial management, human resources, historian—the list goes on. In the early days, I never considered hiring people to fill these roles. There was the strain of cash, of course.

In the early days, I struggled to part with money to outsource tasks when every penny counts. That decision is also a lot, and perhaps even more, about the mindset I had around those roles and tasks. I felt more responsible having at least a basic understanding of what was happening in my business in an effort to better understand where I currently was and where, eventually, I wanted Verano to be.

I'll admit: part of this hesitation to let things go was because I didn't want to be duped. I came from a place of fear: What if someone takes advantage of me? What if I pay them to handle this, and then I don't know enough about that aspect

of my business to know if they're doing a good job or not? This lack of trust combined easily with tight finances to make a situation in which I felt very comfortable keeping every task and every role to myself. Why not? I could easily work eighteen-hour days, I was doing a great job of selling, and I was able to watch every single aspect of my business.

Then I grew up a bit, and I found some accountability partners in my network who were also growing their businesses. I looked at the women in my community who were doing what I wanted to be doing, and I observed what their businesses looked like. No one—not a single one—did everything on their own. They all formed teams of some variety and to handle some portion of the workload. I learned about $15 per hour tasks and $150 per hour tasks: if you want to pay yourself $150 per hour, don't do the tasks you can pay others to do for $15 per hour.

AND THEN.

Then I got pregnant, and a lot of things changed. My energy dipped. My desire to stay awake and work late hours was still there, but my physical ability to do so simply was not. I was zapped, and I knew I had to look at my business a bit differently than before. I couldn't be the "hero" all the time. It was time for a change.

The best thing I ever did, and the first thing I did when deciding how to build a team, was to do a "brain dump" of all the tasks I did for an entire week of my business. I kept a simple sheet of white paper on my desk at all times, and during the day, I would jot down everything I did. I reviewed it at the

end of the day to double-check that I captured everything, and then I would triple-check it to make sure that all of the phone calls, meetings, and client conferences were accounted for. At the end of the week, I had amassed a shocking list of the things I was doing to keep my business thriving.

The list was impressive: it actually provided me relief. No wonder I was exhausted! I was taking care of hundreds of things in a week, and that list didn't account for so many other things. Want to know what wasn't on the list? Every time I laced up my shoes and took my dog for a jog and spent the time thinking through a client's challenge. Or the time I would spend chatting casually with Adam about who else I could reach out to and how else I could grow my business. The conversations with my parents about what I was doing for clients in an effort to help them spread the word with their own networks and communities. None of the stress, the pride, the worry were reflected, but hours and hours and hours of work were written right there on that piece of paper.

Making that list did one simple thing for me: it put into black and white the multitude of things I was carrying on my own. The list was crazy, and there was no way I could ignore it now. Having that physical reminder of everything that was constantly floating around in my head was powerful.

I sat back in my office chair and stared at the list a little while longer. My IKEA desk was covered with client files. I could see that it was a beautiful day. My office at the time was perfect. I took a few minutes to just watch the shadows that the leaves made on my carpet. It was a good reminder that I knew the sunshine was there, but I hadn't actually been outside to

feel it on my skin yet. I had been working all day, enjoying the sunshine through shadows on my floor.

I considered the impact that having a baby was going to have on this list in particular, and my life in general. How, exactly, was I supposed to do all of these things on my list while also learning how to be a mother?

The truth was clear. I can't do it all on my own—parenting or business. And the good news is I'm lucky to not have to. I had a husband who was nervously excited to be a dad. And I had an entire community of people who had their own businesses offering exactly the services I needed.

I opened up to the idea of bringing other people into my business who *wanted* to support me and were experts at what they did. I started outsourcing, very slowly. I picked up my scribbled list of tasks, and I picked one thing that I needed to get off my plate. That one thing I picked was accounting and taxes. I was not an expert, and frankly, managing finances in my business took a significant amount of energy and caused a lot more anxiety than anything else I was doing. I hired a bookkeeper, and I found an accountant that specialized in helping solo entrepreneurs. As it turns out, I LOVE paying them for their help. It was a financial leap of faith at first. Could I spare the money every month?

Paying an expert pays off. The hard-earned cash I spend on a bookkeeper and an accountant to help manage my business's funds and compliance is the best money I spend every month. I don't even think twice about the bills—I'm happy to pay them and take that worry off my plate. I know my books are

clean. I trust the people I work with, and I know enough about what I'm looking at to feel competent, but certainly not an expert. The mental lightening is enough to be worth it, but I get the actual work product, too. They're experts, and they can handle it.

That's the thing: we don't NEED to be experts in all the areas of our businesses. This is an area in which a lot of my fellow business owners get stuck: feeling the need to do it all. There are books and podcasts and websites and loads of articles with data and statistics that actually show us that *doing it all* does not actually do anything for our businesses.

If you are feeling this, know 1) you are not alone and 2) you do not need to run a business alone!

Your own process for hiring a team may look different than mine. Before AJ, my first daughter, was born, I had three people who helped me: my accountant, my bookkeeper, and my husband. Before Lena, my second daughter, was born three and a half years later, I had no fewer than:

- A business assistant
- A retainer writer
- Two freelance writers
- A retainer graphic designer
- Two freelance graphic designers
- A freelance website designer
- A retainer social media specialist
- An accountant
- A bookkeeper
- At least one intern

- A personal coach
- A mastermind/accountability group

The last three roles were not always paid, but they were critical to my growth and well-being. I made more money in 2019 when Lena was born than I did in 2016 when AJ was born, but I wasn't making fifteen times more money between those years in order to be able to afford fifteen more people to support my business. I simply learned to value the expertise of others and see their impact on my life. With their help, I was able to be a bit more available as a mom, wife, friend, colleague, and account manager. Honestly, I was a bit more available to simply *be*.

You are going to need help if you want your business to continue and also give yourself time and space away from work to recover from birth, get to know your baby, and adjust to motherhood—and this is true for first babies as well as their little brothers and sisters. Practice outsourcing tasks well before your planned due date. Give yourself as much time as possible to get to know your team, and start to take things off your plate as much as you can as early as you can.

- Make a brain dump of all of your tasks.
- Explore which tasks you find the most draining or that weigh the heaviest on your mind.
- Get multiple quotes for outsourcing that task, or even part of that task in your business
- Build the budget. It's likely that the money is there! Consider the $15 per hour versus $150 per hour approach.
- Be patient with training and onboarding. This can be the hardest part!

> **$15 per Hour vs. $150 per Hour Work**
> There are a lot of versions of this thought-work available in the world. Here's the one that clicked for me. If you were to look at your day, you have a finite set of hours. Deciding how to spend those hours can be a challenge. And just because you CAN keep your own books clean doesn't necessarily mean you SHOULD. For instance, in my case, would I pay someone else $150 per hour to clean up my QuickBooks account? Not likely. Is someone else willing to pay me $150 per hour to create their business' content strategy for a new product? Yes, they are. So why would I spend an hour doing a $15 per hour task when I should be spending it on a $150 per hour task?

Look at your task list and see what you could outsource for less money than what you would need to pay yourself to complete that task. Can you knock out a social media calendar in thirty minutes? Great—go for it! If that calendar takes you two days and still doesn't flow the way you want it to, find someone to help. Your time is better spent on something else. An exception to this is those tasks that keep your energy flowing and your fire burning in your business. Hang on to those tasks at all costs!

Note: This is for explanation purposes only! I clearly think bookkeepers are amazing and worth every penny.

CREATING SYSTEMS

"What would happen if you were hit by a bus on your way home?"

My business insurance agent stared at me as I stared at him in horror. *Hit by a bus?!* It felt dramatic, but his point was very clear: if I removed myself from my business, would there be a business left?

The need to develop systems isn't limited to pregnancy. We need systems to help run our businesses and households. We already have hundreds of systems at play, even when things are chaotic. For some moms, *chaos is the system.* Letting dishes and toys sit in the sink and on the floor is the system they use to ensure everyone is in bed and gets a good night's sleep. It works for them and for a certain period of time.

In business, systems help us define how we do certain tasks, handle requests, address customer service problems, market our businesses, and more. There's a system to nearly everything, and *the lack of a system IS a system.* If we don't put more structure in place, the inmates start running the asylum. Without some procedures, templates, protocols, and workflows, our businesses can feel out of control very quickly.

Have you ever thought to yourself: *I know the system. It's in my head and I have it memorized to perfection.* That's great, but to my insurance agent's point: what happens if you're suddenly not there and someone else needs to step into your business? Let's just play pretend for a moment. Let's say you're expecting a baby. And you can't control your unborn child, despite your best efforts. And your baby grows healthily and quickly and decides he's ready to hit the streets of the world four weeks earlier than you planned. THAT HAPPENS ALL THE TIME. This is not a drill!

In the book *Built to Sell: Creating a Business That Can Thrive Without You*, author John Warrillow explains the importance of systems by modeling them in an imaginary graphic design business. Part of his message is simply that businesses that are fully dependent on one person or one person's network are incredibly difficult to sell for any value worth mentioning. The reason is that they lack systems. The main player—you—is the value of the business. If you're not there, there's no business.[69]

So although we're not talking about selling our businesses, we are talking about the need to build a business that works without you, even for a matter of time. I know that for my business, a lot of what people are purchasing is access to me and my experience. While I was planning for each of my daughters' arrivals, I spent the majority of my pregnancy building systems and outsourcing work.

If you've taken the practice of doing the brain dump described in the "Team Planning and Outsourcing" section, you might be able to see the areas of your business that need systems. For most of us, they fall into the following categories:

- **Client and Customer Management:** How do you onboard new clients? Where do you save their information? How do you organize emails and communication from clients?
- **Finances:** How and when do you send invoices? What are your payment terms? How do you handle late payments? How do you organize your expenses? When do you take money out for your own payments and taxes?

---

69 John Warrillow, *Built to Sell* (New York: Penguin, 2010).

- **Legal:** Do you have contracts in place with clients? Do you have employee paperwork completed correctly?
- **Marketing:** How do you track marketing efforts? How do you measure success? How often do you send emails, post on social, write blogs, and attend networking events?
- **Operations:** What are your services? How do you perform your services? Are your services repeatable and consistent? Do they come in packages? How do you start a new project? How do you conclude a client relationship?
- **Personnel:** Who is your team? How often are they paid? Who manages communication? Where do you communicate with your team?
- **Sales:** How do you attract new business? How do you price your services? How do you track what's happening with current prospects?

There are many systems that exist in every business, and the questions above are just the surface. If they feel overwhelming, that's okay. Focus on the aspects of your business that will be essential to handle while you're out and begin there. For me, the most important systems were managing incoming client emails, creating new deliverables based on client feedback, and clear and prompt communication among team members in my absence.

I took one of my CEO days that I planned during my first trimester to simply write out what creating a system looks like. It included determining the person responsible for the work, the if/then system of what to do with feedback, and a chart of who the work needed to go to next based on the type of request we got.

For instance, my executive assistant, Lindsay, who I hired specifically for maternity leave, would check my incoming emails. She would take the client information and feedback on existing projects and assign it to either Lauren, my primary writer, Jessie, my primary designer, or Kacey, my social media manager. They would complete the task and resubmit it to Lindsay, who would submit it to the client in turn. This system ensured that active clients' projects continued uninterrupted. I chose to keep doing the billing, but I had a bookkeeper and my accountant working as usual. Outside of my analysis of the work being completed and managing my own email, Verano was business as usual while I was on maternity leave.

PIPELINE OF WORK

Late in my second trimester, I had a client fully back out of our signed agreement. Their California office was being closed by their Korean headquarters, and my working contract with them was part of the collateral damage. My instant reaction was to panic: $2,200 each month was going to disappear.

The loss of income generated a chain reaction of thoughts. *Do I replace that income?* I knew my sales cycle was between six and eight weeks long. If I started right away, best case scenario was that I would have a couple of weeks working with the client before being out on maternity leave, not considering additional time out of the office for the upcoming Thanksgiving holiday.

How you want to treat your pipeline is worth considering in the second trimester. On one hand, everything I knew about the momentum of my business told me to continuously nurture potential clients throughout my pregnancy in an effort to keep leads coming in after the baby was born. On the other hand, based on how I ran my business and the systems I had in place, I knew I wanted to be involved with each new client I brought into Verano. The decision to remain involved meant I needed to calculate when to stop taking on new business and, in turn, scale back my client nurturing process.

For me, there was a lot of fear of losing the momentum I had worked so hard to gain. What would happen during those eight to ten weeks I was out of the office?

The answer wasn't clear in the moment. Looking back, you can more easily see the truth: you decide. You decide what is going to happen in those weeks you're out. If you want to continue nurturing clients before, during, and after your maternity leave, you can do that. There are so many tools and platforms available to schedule blog posts, social media, newsletters, and other efforts. You can plan networking meetings and lunches before your baby is born, and you can schedule new meetings with folks for when you return.

Similarly, with incoming work, I was not going to turn a new client away because I was going to be out of the office for maternity leave. It took some bravery and a lot of encouragement from my mastermind group, but I created a wait list. New, incoming clients who wanted to work with me would be put on a wait list for when I returned. The imposter

syndrome flared immediately: who would want to wait two or three months to work with me?

As it happened, several clients did. They congratulated me on the upcoming arrival of a new baby and told me to reach out when I was back in the office. One client even offered to put down a deposit. This was mind-blowing to me! But it worked: it offered me the confidence to know I had clients ready and willing to work with me when I was ready to work with them, and that money and work would still be there after my maternity leave.

Here are a few of the important questions to consider during your second trimester regarding your pipeline of work:

- When do you plan to be out of the office for your maternity leave? *Friendly reminder that babies come when babies come sometimes. My little one was a full week early, and that feels like a long time when you weren't planning on it!*
- Do you want new business to begin while you're out? Do you have the systems built for that?
- How long is your sales cycle? In other words, how long does it take for you to either get a yes or no from a prospective client?
- What type of outbound communication do you want to happen while you're out, if any? How will you handle incoming leads during your maternity leave?

COMMUNICATING WITH CLIENTS

Outside of my sweat-inducing anxiety over telling my renewing client I was expecting a baby, communicating with the rest of my clients was a fairly straightforward process. Adam and I decided we would share our happy news with all of our friends and family by fifteen weeks. After that, we were free to share the news with whoever we wanted, clients included. Adam is not particularly active on social media (although he did have a wonderful series of posts called #ponytailchronicals that captured how he styled our daughter's hair every day), so any public messaging would come from me.

There's no rhyme, reason, or requirement when it comes to communicating with clients. But at some point, you'll need to make a decision about who to tell, when to tell them, and what you want to communicate. I primarily communicated with active clients on the phone, and then I included the news in a general Verano newsletter. The reaction was overwhelmingly positive, and I loved the process of bringing people into my personal life.

When I spoke with current clients, I was proactive in answering a handful of questions:

- When was I planning to begin my maternity leave?
- What was the process while I was out?
- Who would their primary contact be?
- Did this impact anything in our existing relationship?
- When would they like to have a planning session?

I set up planning sessions with every client. The goal was to get very clear about what deliverables needed to be completed

before I was out on leave. My maternity leave was going to coincide with the end of the year, which was a nice clean break for wrapping up some projects. For clients whose work was going to continue on while I was out, the planning session was used to introduce them to the team member who was going to handle their account and discuss what the expectations were in that time. The planning sessions were equally helpful for the clients and for the Verano team and me.

PLANNING AHEAD

Continue to schedule CEO days. If you can, add more. The closer you get to your due date, the more you'll need to spend time working on your business: creating systems, training team members, scheduling outbound marketing, and more. I found Fridays to be great days for CEO days, as most clients have fewer requests on Fridays and I like the energy and momentum heading into my weekends.

The second trimester is a great time for these high-intensity activities and making decisions. For most women, the second trimester is the best in terms of feeling good and reduced morning sickness. Take advantage of the time to dig into your business!

20

The Third Trimester

The sound of dragging furniture on a hardwood floor is enough to make any homeowner cringe. I was thirty weeks pregnant with Lena, our second child, and staring down the hallway of the second floor of our home in late September. My husband was away at a golf tournament for the weekend, so I took advantage of the time at home by myself to make some executive decisions about how to use the rooms upstairs in our house. I was trying to envision how and where to set up my home office for a maternity leave, plus we needed to create a room for the baby.

I could feel my body slowing down and getting more uncomfortable as the baby grew bigger. This was my chance to rearrange furniture the way I wanted it done, or risk never doing it at all. The way I had things set up after this particular weekend was sure to be the way the furniture would stay for a long time—and definitely until the baby was born. Adam was getting a final competitive golf tournament in for the season, and he was due for shoulder surgery in a month. After that, we would be counting down the days until the

baby was born. When it came to rearranging rooms, it was now or never.

I knew it didn't *truly* matter how the furniture was set up, but I was in the nesting phase and determined to get things just right. I spent time pacing the rooms to determine what my life might look like once our second daughter was born. Would I want to rock her in one corner or the other? Where is the morning sun? Where would I be able to take a conference call quietly if the baby was sleeping?

Planning my maternity leave was becoming more and more real. First, there was no option but to notice my body when I saw my own reflection. The changes were obvious: this baby was growing and my body was responding as needed. Second, my brain started to fizzle out more. I found myself daydreaming about cuddling up with my daughter, who was due the first week of December, and watching Hallmark holiday movies for an entire month.

Client work felt less urgent, and I couldn't help but spend more time thinking about my upcoming maternity leave. Looking back, this shift feels obvious, but at the time I didn't notice how dramatically my thoughts had shifted. I felt like I had exhausted all of my work energy during the second trimester while I implemented systems, trained new hires, communicated with clients, and set expectations across the board. The only time I had any creativity left was when envisioning the near future—the reason I had worked so diligently for the last six months.

The third trimester was all about transitioning. I was physically feeling very pregnant, and that was increasing by the day. Those physical changes impacted my mental and emotional state and served as a constant, tangible reminder that my life was going to change whether or not I was ready. With a due date nearing, I starting thinking more realistically about how to transition from before to after. This included thoughts about the space around me as well as logistics like handing off accounts to my team and removing myself from the conversation. Most of my energy naturally went to planning for the birth and immediately thereafter, and it took more concentrated effort to stay focused on the here and now:

Third Trimester Focus:

- Physical Changes
- Future Work Needs: When, Where, and How
- Transitioning Work to Team Members

PHYSICAL CHANGES

The pregnancy glow was, for me, the biggest lie about pregnancy. I truly never felt that ethereal power that many women claim during their pregnancies. Both pregnancies primarily left me feeling enormous, tired, and uncomfortable. I am very grateful to be able to carry babies in my body, but I didn't love being pregnant. The physical changes were hard for me, and they impacted both my work and home lives.

One of the best aspects of being an Expectant Entrepreneur had nothing to do with running my own calendar or working from home on the days I felt particularly tired. My favorite aspect of being an Expectant Entrepreneur was the ability to

wear anything I wanted to work—and at this point in time, it was all comfort, all the time.

"Do you mind if I turn up the air conditioning a notch?"

My business partner, Rachel, was practically shivering at her desk in the Space Community Workplace, the offsite meeting space we co-owned. I was freezing her out of her own work environment. My pregnant body in the summer months was a furnace like no other: I ran our air conditioning at a crisp sixty-eight degrees and still felt warm when I moved around (which was getting more difficult by the day).

On any given day, I could be found wearing athletic shoes or sandals, maternity leggings, and a t-shirt. On "fancy" days, maternity jeans and a nicer t-shirt ere my MO. My hair stayed in ponytails and messy buns for most of 2019, as blow drying and curling my hair was simply too much to do on a regular basis.

And the best part? My business was totally fine.

I was appropriately dressed when I needed to be. But on days I was simply working on client work, hosting phone calls, or diving into my own business operations, I was all comfort all the time. Tight pants and painful feet are the fastest way to stifle creativity, and they had to go. I'm convinced this decision was what ultimately helped my business work best in my third trimester. I wasn't distracted by discomfort in my wardrobe, I could easily go for a walk when I wanted or needed to relieve tension, and my morning routine was simple and straightforward.

The third trimester can and will be different for everyone, but use your business to your advantage. Verano operates as a fairly casual business in normal times. During pregnancy, I made my own rules and I abided by them: wear what works. No painful shoes, no pants that dig. Done.

As your body grows and changes and demands more from you, find ways to adapt your business to encourage healthy pregnancies. I slept later in the morning and adjusted my very early start time to a more normal hour of the day to allow for better sleep. Lunch breaks, nap breaks, late-night work sessions are key while baby is moving around. Your physical changes are likely to feel the most significant during the third trimester, so work with your body as best you can.

FUTURE WORK NEEDS: WHEN, WHERE, AND HOW
Will you send baby to day care?

Will he or she have a sitter or nanny?

When will you work?

Where will you work?

How will you work?

As much as I love my children, I generally loved getting back to work after my maternity leaves. With my first daughter, I spent about five dedicated weeks figuring out how to be a mom and spending time with her. My itch to return to work was there, but I also *had* to get back to work. I didn't know

as much about what to expect with a new baby (what new mom does?), and my assumption was that I'd be ready to hit the ground running after a month or so. My transition back to work was simultaneously a relief from the demands of a newborn and a very hard process. I was excited to get back into my own identity, but I had not thought through where, when, or how I was going to work. Adam and I had sold our first home and moved into an apartment in anticipation of buying a new house.

For several weeks, I tried to work in the apartment. I set up a small desk in the main living area. My work environment really only needs to include a laptop and some headphones, so I had the luxury of being mobile. This setup worked for about forty-five minutes. The first time I took a conference call, AJ was crying her newborn cry in the background. Adam felt confined to our bedroom in an effort to give me a quiet space to work. I resented the fact that I was sitting at a desk while he was laying with our baby, who I couldn't help but miss even though I found newborns exhausting.

I need to get out of here.

My thought was simply to remove myself from our apartment. Our complex had a business space with gorgeous high-top tables, fast Wi-Fi, and a small TV for background noise. I moved my "office" there. That lasted about two days. The barstool-style seats and high-top tables were beautiful, but working at them for more than an hour or two was physically uncomfortable. Two or three other people also liked to work in this space, and my new-mom hormones had me feeling annoyed by their phone calls and general presence.

I moved up to the lounge area on the top floor of our building. I sat on the deep blue suede couches, which were much preferable to the backless stools of the work area, but there weren't many electrical outlets to charge my laptop. The glamorous room was beautiful to look at, but all of the metal and empty surfaces made a less-than-optimal echo chamber for my conference calls.

This is the worst.

I was two floors away from my baby, but I felt like I couldn't be near her for the sake of being in "work mode." Yet I couldn't find a place to really get into a productive flow. My client roster was good, but it took a dip while I was out on my first maternity leave. Money was tighter than usual, but I had to change my environment. I took a walk around my neighborhood and scanned for "Office Space Available" signs. After a few phone calls, I found an open unit within walking distance from my apartment that was run down, but quiet and had reliable Internet. I signed the agreement that day and moved my stuff in the following morning.

The physical environment matters. If you are a nursing mom, finding a place to pump and store milk is essential, or finding a place to work at home that truly allows you to work between breastfeeding sessions. I had supply issues, and both of my daughters were formula-fed, which ended up being a wonderful thing for our family, but I watch many other moms struggle to find clean, comfortable places to pump or feed their babies. It will impact how you work, so think about it now.

"It feels like our home is always shifting," said Shawna Navaro, owner of Innerspace creative design company. "I struggled sometimes with finding kid-free space to create a home office that would give me the physical space I needed to get work done when I have the opportunity to do so."

Will you be the one staying home with your baby? Will you send your baby to day care or have a nanny? The third trimester is when all of these things need to come together. Hopefully, your discussions about finances in the first trimester included some of these decisions. These last few months of pregnancy are when you need to ensure that you're on a wait list for a day care facility or have a particular sitter on the calendar for after your baby is born. Even if you don't plan to do anything until the baby is a few months old, finding a spot in the day care you like can take some time, so think ahead, make your calls, and envision what you want that return to work to look like.

Similarly, having some thoughts now about the transition period between being home and on maternity leave and returning to work can be very impactful. I reduced a lot of my return-to-work anxiety with my second daughter by simply preparing my home office for work. By this time, we had moved into our home. I knew that there would be some weeks that I wanted to work, but I wasn't ready to leave the house and go back to my outside office yet. I arranged my home office to better suit a work-from-home situation, and I stocked up on work materials like paper and file folders just to have them ready. These are easy to order online and have delivered to you, but having them ready at home in advance made me feel a bit more prepared.

The transition to work can be nebulous for all of us: there's no rule about when you need to go back to work like there is in the corporate world. I found that most of the women I knew starting really thinking about work three to four weeks after the baby was born and returned to work by ten weeks. This is due, in my opinion, to the fact that as business owners, we think about our businesses all the time and they are a part of who we are. I found the newborn phase to be very disorienting and overwhelming, and returning to the part of my identity of business owner helped me feel confident and in control. But with proper planning and good systems in place, your maternity leave can last as long as you want it to! That's the beauty of being in an Expectant Entrepreneur: you can plan and prepare for the life that you want.

Some of the important questions to answer about your return to work include:

- When do you want to go back to work?
- Where will you work when it's time to go back?
- Do you have an environment that is truly conducive to working with a baby around?
- How often will you work? Five days a week? Three? Remember: this is your business, so you get to decide!
- Do you need to budget for some changes, like a new office space or different work equipment (like a mini fridge for storing breast milk)?

TRANSITIONING WORK TO TEAM MEMBERS

"Lauren will be your main point of contact for your project starting next week."

This one sentence was potentially one of the most powerful sentences I wrote in 2019—and I'm a writer. That sentence reflects so much more than you might think after a quick sur-face-read. The only reason I was able to write that sentence to my clients was because I had worked so hard for eight months to *make sure* I could write that sentence. I had hired the right people, trained them to be comfortable with the systems in my business, communicated clear expectations with my team and also with my clients, and—most importantly—learned to let go of control.

When it came down to it, the final handoff was not a big deal. It was a single email introduction between the client and the person on my team who would be handling their account. But it reflected *everything* I had worked so hard to plan and prepare. Every time I wrote that sentence, I couldn't believe it was there. The work was done! My business was going to move forward, and the transfer of responsibility was in process.

I started those emails in mid-November. My due date with Lena was the first week of December. I wanted to buffer the transition slightly to give my Verano team time to work out any blips in the systems and have me readily available for questions that might come to the surface.

The morning I went into labor, which was the Friday after Thanksgiving, I was particularly thankful that we made the transitions when we did. I had my daughter a week before her due date. Had we waited until the first week of December, the transitions would have been hurried and done from a hospital bed via my cell phone. Instead, I got to send a happy

text to my team letting them know the baby was here and everyone was, thankfully, doing quite well. It was time for them to work independently, and they did just that.

"It's hard to bring people into your business, but I'm getting better at it," said Samantha Leenheer, owner of Samantha Joy Events. "As a business owner, we just don't always ask for help."

Slowing down enough to develop the systems, train the team members, document the processes, and communicate everything to the right people can be hard. That is not easy work. In my experience, it was worth every frustration. The best part about transitioning work is that you do not have to transfer it back. I'll say it again: *you do not need to transfer work back to yourself.* All of the planning, preparing, and organizing persists beyond your maternity leave.

Team members don't vanish. Systems don't disappear. Optimizing your business to run without you means that your business can run without you. When you return to work, you can capitalize on all of these transitions and reenter as CEO if you want to. Take the time you created for yourself and hold onto it!

Part 4

The Fourth Trimester

21

Returning to Work— and Beyond

———

Congratulations, mama!

The fourth trimester is the three months that follow the birth of your baby. In my experience, this was the most challenging time for me with each of my girls. Not only is your body undergoing some intense recovery from birth, but you're also now caring for a newborn baby. Between the feedings and lack of sleep and getting to know your new child, the fourth trimester can be incredibly intense.

It's a good thing you planned for it!

Here's the thing about a newborn: they command your attention, whether you're prepared for it or not. As a person who tends to prepare in advance, I still had loose ends and things that popped up during both of my maternity leaves. I would handle them as best I could, but in all honesty, I struggled to think clearly about work at all during those first few months,

especially in the first five to six weeks. Regardless of whether you planned for a maternity leave, your body and your baby will likely demand all of the attention and focus you can muster. Anything leftover tends to be absorbed by taking care of your other children if you have them, updating friends and family, doctors' appointments, and self-care. And that's exactly how it should be!

As an entrepreneur, part of my self-care was thinking about my business. These thoughts usually started to pop up about six weeks after each of my girls was born. In those six weeks leading up to that time, business carried on just like I planned for it. But I started to want to check my email, get a sense of how projects were moving forward, and connect with my business friends again. I wanted to share the good news and begin to integrate my business and my family together.

Baby steps were all I could manage at first, but it felt better to me to spend thirty minutes a day checking emails and touching base with team members. Otherwise, my mind would wander and the feeling of being out of touch with my business caused more anxiety than scanning emails and sending quick updates.

Of course, this is my own brain at work! Six weeks was when I started to feel the itch, but I know plenty of women who felt it earlier, and many others who didn't even have a thought about work until at least ten or twelve weeks. Whatever that time frame is for you, own it. You've planned for it! The last nine months of preparation, planning, and decision-making had just one goal in mind: to help your business move forward while you took as much time as you wanted or needed

after having your baby. This is everything you worked so hard to build—and you get to decide how to move forward from here!

USE THE SYSTEMS YOU BUILT

As you decide how to reenter your business after taking time off, challenge yourself to take a moment to look at your business as an outsider. Are projects moving? Are clients getting the information they need? Are you getting paid? Is your team feeling supported? Are *you* feeling supported?

Rely on those systems! You built them for a reason. If they're working, let them continue to work for you. This is the beginning of a new era of your life and your business: you're now a parent, or you're a parent of more children than you were before. It's a new phase, and there will be new challenges that come with it. You have done the hard work of getting your business to this point, and you may find that you need to rely on your systems, team, and efficiencies more than ever before.

RETURNING TO WORK

The transition from maternity leave to "back at work" can look however you want it to look. If you didn't make those decisions before, or if you are feeling the need to adjust them now that your baby is here and you have a better understanding of what your child needs, you are in control of what to do now. Want to extend your leave? Great! Communicate with your team and rely on those systems for however long you want or need. Anxious to get back to work? Excellent! Let

your team know where and how you plan to get back into operations and how this impacts them.

The most important aspect of returning to work is finding out what's going to work best for you. Of course, our businesses provide money for our lives, so there is going to be a return to work at some point. But it doesn't need to be today, and it doesn't need to be a 100 percent return right away.

Whether you want to resume some aspects of work, like client emails or starting to put out new marketing for your business, or come back more hands-on with client projects and deliverables, you need to communicate with your team. You communicated a plan to them, and if that plan is going to shift, they need to know.

For me, this meant letting some of the people I hired know I would be taking a look at our task management system and assigning some upcoming tasks to myself. The biggest challenge in my business, with everyone working remotely, is ensuring that people have a clear understanding of my expectations for their work. If I was going to change the expectations by absorbing some of the tasks, they needed to be aware of this and know exactly how it affected their work.

I used a simple system in my business:

- First, I communicated directly with the person who was currently handling the task I wanted to take on. This was usually via email as I was still on a weird, baby-dominated sleep-wake cycle and phone calls were hard to plan.

- Second, I would communicate with the client and copy the team member so everyone knew I was back and available. This email included how I planned to be involved and the best way to communicate with me about the project.
- Third, I would check in with the client separately to get an update from their perspective: How did things go? How do they feel about how the project is progressing? This email was my opportunity to let clients bring any issues up or identify any areas of concern OR celebrate the progress and give kudos to my team member.

Slowly, task by task, I put things back on my working plate that I felt ready to handle. But the best and most important thing I ever did for my business was *never* take certain tasks back on. My team had worked hard to get to this point, and there was no need for me to go back to the past of micromanaging everyone. They were working great, and everyone felt happy with the results. My work there was done!

BEYOND THE FOURTH TRIMESTER: CONCLUSION

As you can imagine, going back to work during or after the fourth trimester comes with an entirely new set of questions, narratives, and themes to consider as a working parent. You graduate from the pregnancy-centered part of being an Expectant Entrepreneur into the world of being a business-owning mother. Now, you get to focus on the dream-centered part of being an Expectant Entrepreneur: what else do you expect of yourself, your business, and your life?

As you move into this period of transition, there will be so much more to explore. There will be new questions, new challenges, new victories, and new celebrations. You'll have triumphs and failures as both a parent and a business owner. You will need to make tiny, everyday decisions as well as huge, life-changing ones. And you will do it all with the mindset and tenacity of an Expectant Entrepreneur.

When I set out to create this project, my goal was to let other women know that they are not alone. Everything you're feeling—we feel it, too. I leave you with a reminder that you are not alone on this journey. Even—perhaps *especially*—when you feel like no one in the world knows exactly the pressure you're feeling or the tension that's building between motherhood and business ownership, remember you have a community of women who have successfully navigated this territory before you. And that you, right now, are creating a path that another woman will want to learn from and hear about.

We are your community. Share this book. Tell your story to other Expectant Entrepreneurs. Find us online. Create your own group to share, be vulnerable, and create relationships for business and personal support. Your story matters, and we want to learn from it!

Finally, know that you are capable and talented and a wonderful mother and powerful entrepreneur all day, every day.

Congratulations, mama. You did it.

Acknowledgements

I'd like acknowledge those women who gave of their time and personal experience to help support my vision:

Rachel DesRochers, Marie Englesson, Megan Flatt, Maria Friström, Elisabeth Galperin, Katie Garry, Genna Gardner, Clair Jones, Nikki Laub, Samantha Leenheer, Caroline Maurer, Nana Moore, Rachel Murphy, Shawna Navaro, Leah Neaderthal, Jill Salzman, and Dawn Schwartzman

I'd also like to acknowledge with gratitude and appreciation everyone who supported my presale campaign:

Alicia Manson

Ana Moeddel

Andi Evans

Andrea L Whitley

Andrea Backscheider

Andy Lorenz

Ann Levelle

Anne Behm

Beth Martino	Bette Hackett
Brigid Tremblay	Cady North
Caitlin Wall	Celia McCoy
Chelsea Lay	Chris Geiger
Christina Stranges	Colleen O'Connor
Connie Kreutzjans	Danielle Henry
Dawn Schwartzman	Dennis Hackett
Dr. Eleanor Glass	Eleanor Mueller
Elisabeth Galperin	Emerald Sparks
Emily Baute	Emily C. Morgan
Emily Ryan	Eric Koester
Erin Hackett	Erin Krawsczyn
Erin Navaro	Genna Gardner
Geraldine Harbison	Ghada Alrefia
Gregory Flasch	Gretchen Wilson
Hannah Byam	Heather M Rubacky

Jenn Robertson

Jessica Smith

Julie Gott

Karen Aerts

Kathleen Anderson

Katie Garry

Kristine Kolzing

Lauren Pax

Linda Aumiller

Lindsey Alexander

Margaret Mueller

Maria Fristroem

Marisa M. O'Neill

Mary Guthrie

Meghan Donnellon Hyden

Mickey Irizarry

Jenna Heck

Jessie Ford Coots

Kacey King Redmond

Katherine Preede

Katie Bachmeyer

Kimberly Navaro

Lauren Ehrler

Leslie A. Young

Lindsay Schwartz

Lynn

Margy Coscia

Marie Englesson

Mary Ennis

Maureen Devine-Ahl

Melanie Booher

Molly Nelson

Morgan Bissell Desrosiers	Nicole Winhusen Daniels
Pamela O'Laughlin	Patty Ryan
Rachel Murphy	Rita Alexander
Sarah Burns	Sarah Dowlin
Shannon Quinn	Sue Krasmer
Tamia tinson	Tammy Kremer
Tara Halpin	Tarek Kamil
Tim & Shawna Navaro	Todd Geers
Tricia Horn	Vincent Homan

Finally, a special thank you to New Degree Press, Eric Koester, my writing partner Nnamdi Nwaezeapu, and my entire editing team for helping make this book a reality.

Appendix

————

1. THE EVOLUTION OF WOMEN'S ROLES

Charatan, Debrah Lee, "30 Years of Female Entrepreneurship: From Anomalies To Assets," *Entrepreneur.com*, May 4 2016. https://www.entrepreneur.com/article/270095.

Codrington III, Wilfred U. and Alex Cohen. "The Equal Rights Amendment Explained." Brennan Center. January 23, 2020. Accessed October 11, 2020. https://www.brennancenter.org/our-work/research-reports/equal-rights-amendment-explained.

Encyclopaedia Britannica Online, s.v. "Women's Rights Movement," accessed October 11, 2020, https://www.britannica.com/event/womens-movement.

Guildren, George. "Women in the Work Force." *The Atlantic,* September 1986. https://www.theatlantic.com/magazine/archive/1986/09/women-in-the-work-force/304924/.

Hochschild, Arlie, and Anne Machung. *The Second Shift: Working families and the revolution at home.* New York: Penguin, 2012.

National Women's History Museum. "Why Are So Many Teachers Women?" Accessed April 11, 2020. https://www.womenshistory. org/articles/why-are-so-many-teachers-women.

Parker, Elaine. "Women Entrepreneurs are on the Rise." *The Hill.* January 19, 2019. https://thehill.com/opinion/civilrights/426157-women-entrepreneurs-are-on-the-rise-lets-continue-the-trend.

Stetson, Grace. "The Untold History Behind Why Most Real Estate Agents Are Women." *Apartment Therapy,* March 30, 2019. https://www.apartmenttherapy.com/women-in-real-estate-history-268098.

United, States. "Public Law 100-533, Women's Business Ownership Act of 1988, 25 October 1988." *Annual review of population law* 15 (1988): 174.

VanderBrug, Jackie. "The global rise of female entrepreneurs." *Harvard Business Review* 4 (2013). https://hbr.org/2013/09/global-rise-of-female-entrepreneurs.

2. THE CHALLENGE OF WOMEN'S ENTREPRENEURSHIP

Bryant, Miranda. "Maternity Leave: US Policy Is Worst on List of the World's Richest Countries." *The Guardian.*January 27, 2020. https://www.theguardian.com/us-news/2020/jan/27/maternity-leave-us-policy-worst-worlds-richest-countries.

Castrillon, Caroline. "Why More Women Are Turning to Entrepreneurship." *Forbes*, February 4, 2019. https://www.forbes.com/sites/carolinecastrillon/2019/02/04/why-more-women-are-turning-to-entrepreneurship/#339693dd542a.

Elting, Liz. "Why Women Quit." *Forbes*, October 21, 2019. https://www.forbes.com/sites/lizelting/2019/08/21/why-women-quit/#44a45f5716fa.

Goffee, Robert and Richard Scase. *Women in Charge: The Experiences of Female Entrepreneurs* (New York: Routledge, 1985), 5.

Hyder, Shama. "State Of Women And Entrepreneurship 2020: Here's What You Need To Know." *Forbes*. March 10, 2020. https://www.forbes.com/sites/shamahyder/2020/03/10/state-of-women-and-entrepreneurship-2020-heres-what-you-need-to-know/#7a4c31b969fa.

Keshner, Andrew. "Child-care costs in America have soared to nearly $10k per year." *MarketWatch*. March 8, 2019. https://www.marketwatch.com/story/child-care-costs-just-hit-a-new-high-2018-10-22.

Light, Paulette. "Why 43% of Women With Children Leave Their Jobs, and How to Get Them Back." *The Atlantic*. April 19, 2013. https://www.theatlantic.com/sexes/archive/2013/04/why-43-of-women-with-children-leave-their-jobs-and-how-to-get-them-back/275134/.

Miller, Claire Cain. "The Motherhood Penalty vs. the Fatherhood Bonus." *The Upshot (Blog)*, *The New York Times*. September 6, 2014. https://nyti.ms/1qDxZeE.

Sarkis, Stephanie. "Gender Inequality Led to the Rise of Women Entrepreneurs." *Forbes,* March 5, 2019. https://www.forbes.com/sites/stephaniesarkis/2019/03/05/gender-inequality-led-to-the-rise-of-women-entrepreneurs/.

Sheng, Ellen, "This underfunded female demographic is launching the most start-ups in America, far from Silicon Valley," *CNBC. com.* February 25, 2020. https://www.cnbc.com/2020/02/25/underfunded-female-demographic-is-launching-the-most-start-ups-in-us.html.

Thomas, Rachel, Ali Bohrer, Marianne Cooper, Ph.D., Jess Huang, Ellen Konar, Ph.d., Alexis Krivkovich, Ava Mohshenin, Irina Starkova, Lareina Yee, Delia Zonischi. *Women in the Workplace 2019.* LeanIn.Org, 2019. Accessed April 20, 2019. https://womenintheworkplace.com/2019.

VanderBrug, Jackie. "The Global Rise of Female Entrepreneurs." *Harvard Business Review.* September 4, 2013. https://hbr.org/2013/09/global-rise-of-female-entrepreneurs.

"Visa 2020 State of Female Entrepreneurship Report." *Visa.* February 2020, 6.

3. DISTINCTION: MOMPRENEURS & MOTHER-ENTREPRENEURS

Abrams, Sandy. "Mompreneurs: Products Made by Moms for Moms." *The Blog, Huffington Post,* December 6, 2017. https://www.huffpost.com/entry/momprenurs-made-by-moms-f_b_3226834.

Betts, Kris. "Mompreneurs: Working from home through 'social commerce." *KVUE.com.* July 7, 2017. https://www.kvue.com/article/news/local/mompreneurs-working-from-home-through-social-commerce/269-454624375.

Downey, Lucas. "Mompreneur." *Investopedia,* August 21, 2018. https://www.investopedia.com/terms/m/mompreneur.asp.

Krystal, "Please Stop Calling Me a Mompreneur," *Daily Femme (blog),* 2017. https://www.dailyfemme.com/please-stop-calling-mompreneur/.

Lexico Oxford Dictionary, Online Ed., s.v. "Mompreneur," accessed March 15, 2020. https://www.lexico.com/en/definition/mompreneur.

4. THE UNIQUE MINDSET OF EXPECTANT ENTREPRENEURS

Bryant, Peter and Elena Ortiz Terán. "Entrepreneurs' Brains are Wired Differently." *Harvard Business Review.* December 19, 2013. https://hbr.org/2013/12/entrepreneurs-brains-are-wired-differently.

Hoekzema, Elseline, Erika Barba-Müller, Cristina Pozzobon, Marisol Picado, Florencio Lucco, David García-García, Juan Carlos Soliva, et al. "Pregnancy Leads to Long-Lasting Changes in Human Brain Structure." *Nature Neuroscience* 20, no. 2 (February 2017): 287–96. https://doi.org/10.1038/nn.4458.

Torgerson, Kate. "What Motherhood Taught this CEO About Starting a Business." Interview by IDEO. May 6, 2020. https://

www.ideou.com/blogs/inspiration/what-motherhood-taught-this-ceo-about-starting-a-business.

5. HALLMARKS AND EMERGENT THEMES

Reva, Rachel. "Confessions of a Pregnant Entrepreneur," *Thrive-Global*, August 1, 2018. https://thriveglobal.com/stories/confessions-of-a-pregnant-entrepreneur/.

6. THE STORIES INSIDE

Gambelin, Anne-Marie. "I didn't expect the loneliness of new motherhood — or the importance of community." *Mother.ly* (blog). February 13, 2019. https://medium.com/motherly/i-didnt-expect-the-loneliness-of-new-motherhood-or-the-importance-of-community-695fce3d65e0.

Markham, Laura quoted in Rachel Bertsche, *The Kids Are in Bed: Finding Time for Yourself in the Chaos of Parenting.* New York: Penguin Press, 2020.

Young Entrepreneurs Council. "Why Professional Networking is the Missing Piece to Your Success." Inc. February 22, 2018. https://www.inc.com/young-entrepreneur-council/why-professional-networking-is-missing-piece-to-your-success.html.

8. CURIOSITY

Berger, Warren. "Question Everything." *Success.* May 16, 2014. https://www.success.com/question-everything/.

"Inspiring Innovation." *Harvard Business Review.* August 2002. https://hbr.org/2002/08/inspiring-innovation.

Park, C. Whan, and V. Parker Lessig. "Students and Housewives: Differences in Susceptibility to Reference Group Influence." *Journal of Consumer Research* 4, no. 2 (1977): 102-10. Accessed March 14, 2020. http://www.jstor.org/stable/2488716.

Sinek, Simon. "How Great Leaders Inspire Action." Filmed September 2009 at TEDxPuget Sound, Puget Sound, WA. https://www.ted.com/talks/simon_sinek_how_great_leaders_inspire_action.

Torgerson, Kate. "What Motherhood Taught this CEO About Starting a Business." Interview by IDEO. May 6, 2020. https://www.ideou.com/blogs/inspiration/what-motherhood-taught-this-ceo-about-starting-a-business.

9. EMPATHY

Decety, Jean, and Philip L. Jackson. "The functional architecture of human empathy." *Behavioral and cognitive neuroscience reviews* 3, no. 2 (2004): 71-100.

Fatemi, Falon. "The Value of Investing in Female Founders." *Forbes.* March 29, 2019. https://www.forbes.com/sites/falonfatemi/2019/03/29/the-value-of-investing-in-female-founders/#7fe6f32e5ee4.

Hoekzema, Elseline, Erika Barba-Müller, Cristina Pozzobon, Marisol Picado, Florencio Lucco, David García-García, Juan Carlos Soliva, et al. "Pregnancy Leads to Long-Lasting Changes

in Human Brain Structure." *Nature Neuroscience* 20, no. 2 (February 2017): 287–96. https://doi.org/10.1038/nn.4458.

Hudson, Paul. "Why the Most Successful Entrepreneurs are the Least Egotistical." *EliteDaily*. September 13, 2013. https://www.elitedaily.com/money/entrepreneurship/why-the-most-successful-entrepreneurs-are-the-least-egotistical.

Korte, Russell, Karl A. Smith, and Cheryl Qing Li. "The Role of Empathy in Entrepreneurship: A Core Competency of the Entrepreneurial Mindset." *Advances in Engineering Education* 7, no. 1 (2018). https://eric.ed.gov/?id=EJ1199603.

11. CREATIVITY

Kim, Kyung Hee. "The Creativity Crisis: The Decrease in Creative Thinking Scores on the Torrance Tests of Creative Thinking." *Creativity Research Journal* 23, no. 4 (October 1, 2011): 285–95. https://doi.org/10.1080/10400419.2011.627805.

Mitchell, Marilyn Price, Ph.D. "Creativity: How Parents Nurture the Evolution of Children's Ideas." *Roots of Action (blog)*. April 10, 2017. https://www.rootsofaction.com/nurturing-childrens-creativity/.

Start Your Business (blog), Business News Daily. "How to Harness Creativity as an Entrepreneur." March 5, 2020. https://www.businessnewsdaily.com/5813-creativity-in-entrepreneurship.html.

13. FOCUS

Berman, Robby. "Women are more productive than men, according to new research." *World Economic Forum.*October 8, 2018. https://www.weforum.org/agenda/2018/10/women-are-more-productive-than-men-at-work-these-days.

Hayzlett, Jeffrey. "Why Focus Is the Number-One Element of Business Success." *Entrepreneur.* September 23, 2015. https://www.entrepreneur.com/article/248563.

Mui, Ylan Qi. "Study: Women with more children are more productive at work." *The Washington Post.* October 30, 2014. https://www.washingtonpost.com/news/wonk/wp/2014/10/30/study-women-with-more-children-are-more-productive-at-work/.

Patel, Neil. "How to Focus On What Matters as an Entrepreneur." *Inc.com,* February 19, 2015. https://www.inc.com/neil-patel/how-to-focus-on-what-matters-as-an-entrepreneur.html.

Torgerson, Kate. "What Motherhood Taught this CEO About Starting a Business." Interview by IDEO. May 6, 2020. https://www.ideou.com/blogs/inspiration/what-motherhood-taught-this-ceo-about-starting-a-business.

Wolfe, Whitney. "40 Entrepreneurs Share Their Secrets to Staying Focused." *Entrepreneur.* Accessed May 22, 2019. https://www.entrepreneur.com/slideshow/286302#12.

14. SELF-AWARENESS

Torgerson, Kate. "What Motherhood Taught this CEO About Starting a Business." IDEO U Webinar, May 6, 2020, https://

www.ideou.com/blogs/inspiration/what-motherhood-taught-this-ceo-about-starting-a-business.

15. RESILIENCE

Marie Englesson. "Meet the Swedish entrepreneur who saw the potential for cosmetics in Tanzania." By Dinfin Mulupi. *Africa Business Insight*, March 31, 2015. https://www.howwemadeitinafrica.com/meet-the-swedish-entrepreneur-who-saw-the-potential-for-cosmetics-in-tanzania/47994/.

16. RISK TOLERANCE

Mayo Clinic. "Miscarriage: Symptoms and Causes." Accessed May 26, 2020. https://www.mayoclinic.org/diseases-conditions/pregnancy-loss-miscarriage/symptoms-causes/syc-20354298.

Rooney, Kristin L, and Alice D Domar. "The Relationship between Stress and Infertility." *Dialogues in Clinical Neuroscience* 20, no. 1 (March 2018): 41–47. https://pubmed.ncbi.nlm.nih.gov/29946210.

Torgerson, Kate. "What Motherhood Taught this CEO About Starting a Business." IDEO U Webinar. May 6, 2020. https://www.ideou.com/blogs/inspiration/what-motherhood-taught-this-ceo-about-starting-a-business.

18. THE FIRST TRIMESTER

Department of Health, Human Services, Washington, DC., Healthy People 2010 (Group), and United States Government Printing Office. "Healthy people 2010: Understanding and

improving health." US Department of Health and Human Services, 2000.

Sincero, Jen. *You are a Badass at Making Money: Master the Mindset of Wealth.* Philadelphia: Penguin, 2017.

U.S. Centers for Disease Control and Prevention, "Trends in Pregnancy-Related Death: Pregnancy Mortality Surveillance System." Accessed May 20, 2020. https://www.cdc.gov/reproductivehealth/maternal-mortality/pregnancy-mortality-surveillance-system.htm?CDC_AA_refVal=https%3A%2F%2Fwww.cdc.gov%2Freproductivehealth%2Fmaternalinfanthealth%2Fpregnancy-mortality-surveillance-system.htm.

19. THE SECOND TRIMESTER

Warrillow, John. *Built to Sell.* New York: Penguin, 2010.

Made in the USA
Las Vegas, NV
10 November 2021